Tales of Love and Terror

Booktalking the Classics, Old and New

by Hazel Rochman

AMERICAN LIBRARY ASSOCIATION

Chicago and London

To Hymie, Danny, and Simon

Hazel Rochman is an assistant editor of the Books for Young Adults section of *Booklist*, ALA's review journal for school and public libraries. She has worked as a journalist in South Africa, as an English teacher in London, and as a young adult librarian in the University of Chicago Laboratory Schools. Rochman holds a master's in education with a specialty in school librarianship from the University of Chicago.

Composed by Ampersand, Inc. in
Itek Palatino on a Digitek
typesetting system.

Printed on 50-pound Glatfelter,
a pH-neutral stock, and bound
in 10-point Carolina cover stock
by Braun-Brumfield, Inc.
∞

Library of Congress Cataloging-in-Publication Data

Rochman, Hazel.
  Tales of love and terror.

  Bibliography: p.
  Includes index.
  1. Book talks.   2. Youth—Books and reading.
3. Children—Books and reading.   4. Public relations—
Libraries.   5. Libraries, Children's—Cultural programs.
6. School libraries—Cultural programs.   7. Bibliography
—Best books—Children's literature.   8. Bibliography—
Best books—Young adult literature.   I. Title.
Z716.3.R68   1987   027.62'6   86-32285
ISBN 0-8389-0463-7

Contents

Preface

For eight years, until 1984, I was a school librarian for grades 7–12 at the University of Chicago Laboratory Schools. I was very fortunate; we had a strong, supportive library faculty who worked closely with teachers, and I was able to visit junior high and high school students often—especially in the English and social studies classrooms—to talk about good books to read for pleasure. Much of what follows is based on my experience with those librarians, teachers, and students.

I started writing about books because of Zena Sutherland. She invited me to join the advisory committee of the *Bulletin of the Center for Children's Books* (whose meetings remain a highlight of my week) and firmly pushed me to review for *School Library Journal* and to write about bringing books and young people together. For a long time I couldn't publish a word without first showing it to her.

I am grateful to Lillian Gerhardt, editor of *School Library Journal,* and her staff for the encouragement, the training, and the forum. Writing my first book review took at least a week. My first article was a disaster; they rejected it, and I learned from that. In a direct sense this book has grown out of my articles in *SLJ,* especially "Booktalking the Classics" (February 1984), "Booktalking Them off the Shelves" (August 1984), and "Best Books of '85: Booktalking Them off the Shelves" (April 1986). It was Book Review Editor Trevelyn Jones who came up with the title "Booktalking Them off the Shelves," which I have adopted for Part 1.

The discussions on *Boy, Story for a Black Night, Alan and Naomi,* and *One-Eyed Cat* are based on the article "Young Adult Books: Childhood Terror" in *Horn Book* (September 1985). The section on *Wuthering Heights* in chapter 3 is based on an article that first appeared in *Illinois Libraries* (July 1986) and was reprinted in *Horn Book* (November 1986).

Part of the discussion of *The Moonlight Man* in the chapter on terror first appeared in the *New York Times Book Review* (March 23, 1986).

Some of my annotations on love in chapter 7 were used as part of *Booklist*'s support material for the YASD/NEH project, "Library-Based Programming in the Humanities for Young Adults" in August 1986.

Since September 1984 I have been an assistant editor in the Books for Young Adults section at *Booklist,* the reviewing journal of the American Library Association, where I am part of a close working community. My thanks to *Booklist*'s editor, Paul Brawley, for his commitment and support and for allowing me to quote from reviews, bibliographies, and articles. As far as I know, I have used only my own work, except where I have cited other reviewers. But when you work with people you respect, it's not always clear where an idea begins and how it develops, and this book owes much to the *Booklist* editors, especially to my Young Adult Books colleagues: editor Sally Estes; assistant editor Stephanie Zvirin; and former editor Barbara Duree.

Bettina MacAyeal, my book editor, has an office one floor below mine. Because she loves the literature—adult and young adult—and knows the readers, she has been an ideal guide.

Roger Sutton and I met in fierce discussion on the Best Books for Young Adults committee of the Young Adult Services Division of ALA. We continue to talk and argue (sometimes we find we've switched sides), and the references to Roger are only a hint of his importance to my work.

Betsy Hearne, editor of the *Bulletin of the Center for Children's Books* at the University of Chicago, made me write this book. She understood what I was doing, and with her gift for integrating the demands of the story and the response of the audience, she helped me to do it better.

A special thanks to my mother, who spent two summers helping me type the manuscript and whose total absorption in a good book, oblivious of domestic mayhem, has been a lasting role model.

Acknowledgments

A note about formal acknowledgments: Permission for quotations or paraphrases of copyrighted material was obtained only for the poetry and short stories or where the quotation was more than a small fraction of the whole.

"Song against Broccoli" from *One Fell Soup or I'm Just a Bug on the Windshield of Life* by Roy Blount, Jr. Copyright © 1976 by Roy Blount, Jr. First appeared in *The Atlantic.* Reprinted by permission of Little, Brown and Co. in association with the Atlantic Monthly Press and International Creative Management.

Excerpts from *Boy* by Roald Dahl. Copyright © 1985 by Roald Dahl. Reprinted by permission of Farrar, Straus and Giroux, Inc., and Murray Pollinger.

Paraphrase from "The Sound Machine" (1949) from *Someone like You* by Roald Dahl. Permission by Alfred A. Knopf, Inc.

Excerpts from "The People Could Fly" from *The People Could Fly* by Virginia Hamilton. Copyright © 1985 by Virginia Hamilton. Reprinted by permission of Alfred A. Knopf, Inc.

"The Snake" by D. H. Lawrence from *The Complete Poems of D. H. Lawrence,* collected and edited by Vivian de Sola Pinto and F. Warren Roberts. Copyright © 1964, 1971 by Angelo Ravagli and D. M. Weekley, Executors of the Estate of Frieda Lawrence Ravagli. Reprinted by permission of Viking Penguin, Inc., and Lawrence Pollinger, Ltd.

Excerpts from *The Ballad of the Sad Café and Collected Short Stories* by Carson McCullers. Copyright © 1936, 1941, 1942, 1950, 1955 by Carson McCullers. Copyright © renewed 1979 by Floria V. Lasky. Reprinted by permission of Houghton Mifflin Company and Barrie and Jenkins, an imprint of Century Hutchinson.

"The Gift" by Ed Ochester from *Dancing on the Edge of Knives.* Reprinted from *Dancing on the Edge of Knives* by Ed Ochester by permission of the University of Missouri Press. Copyright © 1973 by Ed Ochester.

Excerpts from discussion of "The Gift" by Ed Ochester from *Poetspeak*, edited by Paul Janeczko. New York: Bradbury Press, an affiliate of Macmillan, Inc., 1983. Excerpted by permission of the publisher.

Excerpts from the articles "Booktalking the Classics," "Booktalking Them off the Shelves," and "Best Books of '85: Booktalking Them off the Shelves" by Hazel Rochman. Reproduced with permission from *School Library Journal* (February, 1984, August 1984, and April 1986). Copyright © R. R. Bowker Company/Cahners Magazine Division.

Excerpts from *Black Boy* by Richard Wright. Copyright © 1945 by Richard Wright. Reprinted by permission of Harper and Row, Publishers, Inc. and Jonathan Cape, Ltd.

"Love Lines" by Betsy Hearne from *Love Lines: Poetry in Person* and excerpts from Introduction. Copyright © 1987 by Betsy Hearne. Margaret K. McElderry Books. Reprinted with the permission of Atheneum Publishers, Inc.

Part 1

Booktalking Them off the Shelves

1 Sharing the Pleasure

I have learned that the best booktalks are about those books I know and love and want to share with others. Always the emphasis is on pleasure—mine and that of the audience. It's no use preaching about reading. Great books touch feeling and imagination. As readers, we understand passionately about others and are changed; we are moved beyond our narrow selves. And for that engagement to happen, a story must grab us, characters must make us care, situations must be dramatic, language must sing. The booktalk has to show the audience, not that *Wuthering Heights* is good for them, but that it is *about* them.

When I booktalk to junior high and high school students, I know that in every group I have to satisfy a wide range of reading interests and of reading levels. I want to stimulate those who, except for class assignments, aren't reading at all. I want to lure readers to the pleasure of science fiction, and to draw those who read only science fiction (or romance or horror or sports statistics) to the pleasure and power of other books. They don't need me to tell them about paperback romances. But some of the *Sweet Dreams* readers might also be ready for *Jane Eyre*. I nearly always try to include a traditional classic. I want to push the audience a little beyond where they might go on their own.

WHY QUALITY?

To many young readers the classics mean difficult, moralistic tomes in tiny print, with false leather bindings and old-fashioned certainties, without explicit sex or violence or bad language, forced on young people for their improvement by authoritarian adults.

Discussing censorship in *Literature for Today's Young Adults,* Alleen Pace

Nilsen and Kenneth Donelson point out that censors who call for a return to great literature and the classics are often non-readers who assume that "classics have no objectionable words or action or ideas. So much for *Crime and Punishment, Hamlet, Madame Bovary, Anna Karenina,* and most other classics. For censors, the real value of great literature is that it is old, dusty, dull, and hard to read, in other words, good for young people."[1]

In fact, the classics are subversive: they move you to question who you are and how you live. And they survive because they give readers intense pleasure.

There are various kinds of pleasure in reading. We all like books that relax and entertain us, reaffirming our familiar world: the easy comfort of mysteries neatly solved, fast thrillers, romantic endings, expectations satisfied—what writer Margaret Atwood calls the "hot water bottles and thumbsucking" kind of reading.[2] But there is also the pleasure in books that unsettle us; bringing questions, even discomfort, while they entertain; moving us deeply into a new way of seeing ourselves. Kafka said books must "wound and stab us"; they must "affect us like a disaster. . . . A book must be the axe for the frozen sea inside us."[3]

Some books written especially for young people do move us in this way, and they have become classics—the best of Fox, Cormier, Westall, Kerr, Hamilton, and others. Many adult classics, both traditional and contemporary, can reach young people with the same power.

I am not suggesting that we ignore students' popular reading tastes. We need to know what they read and respect it. But we also owe young people something more. Too often booktalks aim only at reluctant readers and deal only with what is immediately accessible to everyone. We are not fostering independent thought by providing books with a narrow and simplistic vision. We are guilty of condescension if we prejudge young people as always out for the quick and superficial. They continually surprise me with their openness, their enthusiastic response to many kinds of writing.

Within a classroom there are various reading levels and various reading interests. Further, enthusiasm for a subject will motivate a student to read advanced material, and the same student may be reading at various levels at the same time. Dorothy Broderick, editor of *Voice of Youth Advocates* (*VOYA*), cites an eleventh-grade girl who likes Robin McKinley,

1. Alleen Pace Nilsen and Kenneth L. Donelson, *Literature For Today's Young Adults,* 2d ed. (Glenview, Illinois: Scott, Foresman, 1985), p. 460.

2. Margaret Atwood, *New York Times Book Review,* June 12, 1983, p. 43.

3. Franz Kafka, Letter to Oskar Pollak, January 27, 1904.

Stephen King, Robin Cook, Charles Dickens, Richard Armour, the d'Aulaires' *Book of Greek Myths,* and Harlequin Romances.[4]

Nilsen and Donelson's discussion of the ongoing quality/popularity debate demonstrates the range of adult views—from those who see popularity as primary, to those who decry using popularity as a major evaluation criterion.[5] As Mary K. Chelton points out in her landmark article, "Booktalking—You Can Do It," most of us fall somewhere in between.[6] Your position also depends on what you mean by "quality." And there is a difference between the books you buy for your library and those you promote and booktalk.

Of course we do not want young people reading a book *because* it is a classic, just so they can tell themselves and others they have read it. We do not want to encourage the status reader described so painfully by Richard Rodriguez in his autobiography, *Hunger of Memory*: In high school he worked his way doggedly through a list of "the hundred most important books of Western Civilization," reading each word of each book but often having to check the book jacket to see what he was reading about.[7] I never label a book a classic when I am telling young people about it, though I sometimes slip in phrases like "if you're a good reader" or "a quick read" to indicate reading level.

Every librarian dreads those mimeographed required "outside reading" lists from teachers who haven't deleted or added a title in twenty years. *VOYA* reprinted one, calling it "The World's Worst 8th Grade Reading List?"[8] In contrast, some of the best teachers I have worked with in promoting reading share their own continuing pleasure in mysteries or light best-sellers—or Dostoyevsky—with their classes and they accept their students' popular reading tastes. They encourage students to talk about *all* the books they enjoy. But they have also asked me to come to their classrooms as often as I possibly could to talk about some high-quality books, new and old, that would interest young people. We know that some students will not read the books I discuss; but nearly everyone enjoys the booktalks and feels the excitement and power of books. And some students are stimulated to read the booktalked titles; they are

4. Dorothy M. Broderick, "On Saying YESS to Youth," speech to Illinois Library Association, Youth Services Section, Oct. 17, 1985. Reprinted in *Illinois Libraries* 68:387-92 (June 1986).

5. Nilsen and Donelson, pp. 411-12.

6. Mary K. Chelton, "Booktalking—You Can Do It," *School Library Journal*, 22:39-43 (April 1976).

7. Richard Rodriguez, *Hunger of Memory: The Education of Richard Rodriguez* (Godine, 1982), p. 64.

8. *VOYA* 7:305 (February 1985).

hungry for suggestions, and they come back for more, and they share their pleasure with the class. The ideal is that combination of acceptance and stimulation.

Young people will find formula romances on their own, in the drugstore or on the library display racks. But we are limiting their choices if we do not offer more than is promoted by mass marketing.[9] Author-illustrator David Macaulay, speaking at the ALA–Children's Book Council program on "Books for All Ages" in Los Angeles in 1983, put it this way: library users should be "encouraged to discover what they didn't even know they needed."

Today's young people should not be deprived of what has moved generations of readers. Booktalking about Big Brother in *1984*, or White Fang in the northern wilderness, or Cathy and Heathcliff running wild on the moors in defiance of convention and brutality, can fire the imagination and open up possibilities of feeling and wonder.

Why does everybody know about the scene where Oliver Twist asks for more? Not because Dickens improves the vocabulary, but because (as he says in the book's preface) he writes about "The cold wet shelterless midnight streets."

A brief introduction and read-aloud from *Oliver Twist* is superb entertainment that holds almost any group spellbound:

Starving, beaten and desperate, the boys in a brutal orphanage decide they will ask for more food.

> A council was held; lots were cast who should walk up to the master after supper that evening, and ask for more; and it fell to Oliver Twist.
>
> The evening arrived; the boys took their places. The master, in his cook's uniform, stationed himself at the copper; his pauper assistants ranged themselves behind him; the gruel was served out; and a long grace was said over the short commons. The gruel disappeared; the boys whispered each other, and winked at Oliver; while his next neighbours nudged him. Child as he was, he was desperate with hunger, and reckless with misery. He rose from the table; and advancing to the master, basin and spoon in hand, said: somewhat alarmed at his own temerity:
>
> "Please, sir, I want some more."
>
> The master was a fat, healthy man; but he turned very pale. He gazed in stupefied astonishment on the small rebel for some seconds, and then clung for support to the copper. The assistants were paralysed with wonder; the boys with fear.
>
> "What!" said the master at length, in a faint voice.
>
> "Please, sir," replied Oliver, "I want some more." [ch. 2]

---

9.   See Lillian L. Shapiro, "Quality or Popularity? Selection Criteria for YAs," *School Library Journal* 24:23–27 (May 1978).

Even if many in the class will never read the book, the read-aloud and sharing have the impact of storytelling, communicating a sense of the power and exhilaration of books.

READING ALOUD

The easiest—and often, the most effective—way to booktalk a classic is to combine telling with reading aloud. This applies to many powerfully written books: the author's own words may be the best lure to the world of the story. Holding the book and reading from it, rather than reciting, avoids the tediousness and strain of memorizing. It also communicates your essential message: This pleasure comes from reading.

As in the example of *Oliver Twist*, I introduce the basic situation, lead into a dramatic scene or incident or character, and then let the book speak for itself.

I choose the passage very carefully. In most cases I keep the read-aloud short. I make sure that I know it well, so that I do not lose eye contact with the audience.

Sometimes I link together several passages, as in Meredith Pierce's young adult fantasy, *The Darkangel*: The Darkangel is a vampire, and his evil is beautiful and strange. He comes down in a rush of great black wings, and when he opens them, the girl Aeriel

> . . . found she could not move for wonder. Before her stood the most beautiful youth ever she had seen. His skin was pale and white as lightning, with a radiance that faintly lit the air. His eyes were clear and colorless as ice. His hair was long and silver, and about his throat he wore a chain: on fourteen of the links hung little vials of lead . . . [Tor ed., p. 42]

In thirteen of these vials are the imprisoned souls of his once-beautiful wives. One vial is empty, and if he fills that, his power will be absolute. He takes Aeriel to the castle to be servant to his wives. In a tiny, windowless room are thirteen emaciated women.

> Some stood in corners or crouched, leaning back against the walls. Some crawled slowly on hands and knees; one sat and tore her hair and sobbed. Another paced, paced along a little of the far wall. All screamed and cowered at the entrance of the vampyre.

He leaves Aeriel alone with the wraiths, and they press on her:

> "What has he done to you?" cried Aeriel softly, able to keep her revulsion hidden no longer. "You were women once."
>
> "True," said one.

"We were like you."
"But prettier."
"What has he done to you?" cried Aeriel again.
"Drunk up our blood."
"Stolen our souls."
"Torn out our hearts and thrown them to the gargoyles." [p. 55]

THEMES

I never talk *only* about the classics. In most presentations of twelve to fifteen books I use one or two traditional classics, integrating them into a theme booktalk, moving naturally from popular and contemporary young adult and adult books to the classic and back again.

The theme provides unity and concentration. It allows me to integrate a wide range of reading levels, genres, and subjects and to do so unobtrusively. The theme is a way to lure readers to a wider variety of books than they would find on their own.

This doesn't mean that the theme should be emphasized. The focus is on the books, not the theme. I usually start with an overall theme, and then I use quiet links of parallel or contrast as I go along.

Great books are about more than one theme. As chapter 3 shows, you can use a single book in all kinds of talks, depending on your theme, audience, and the other books you are presenting. Richard Wright's *Black Boy* can be used in a talk on biography or the black experience; I also use it with themes of outsiders, terror, and survival. Jack London's *White Fang* is a superb animal story; I also use it in talks on survival, adventure, terror, love, and war.

The next chapter will discuss in practical detail how to booktalk the great tales of love and terror, ghosts and rage, war and survival—both high-quality modern stories and those that have delighted readers for generations.

BOOKS DISCUSSED

Dickens, Charles. *Oliver Twist*. 1838. Adult classic; gr. 8 up
London, Jack. *White Fang*. Macmillan, 1906. Adult classic; gr. 7 up
Pierce, Meredith Ann. *The Darkangel*. Atlantic, 1982; Tor, 1984. YA; gr. 7 up
Rodriguez, Richard. *Hunger of Memory: The Education of Richard Rodriquez*. Godine, 1982. Adult; gr. 9 up
Wright, Richard. *Black Boy*. Harper, 1945. Adult classic; gr. 7 up

2 Selection, Preparation, and Style

I usually take a book truck with me to the classroom. I booktalk twelve or fifteen books for half an hour or so, and then the students come and browse and talk and check out the books right there if they want to. On the lower shelves of the truck I include about thirty other books: duplicates; books in the same genres or by the same authors as those I discuss; books I spoke about last time; good books that provide variety; always a wide range of genres, subjects, reading levels.

In deciding which books to talk about, I try to find out as much as possible about my audience in advance. I know I won't reach them if I talk about books that are too far above or below them in reading level, or if I'm too far removed from what they care about.

Use what they care about. For example, if there's a strong interest in basketball, try Bruce Brooks's *The Moves Make the Man,* which is a dramatic sports story and also a powerful picture of an interracial friendship. Or, if track is a big interest try the classic long short story, *The Loneliness of the Long Distance Runner* by Alan Sillitoe.

In talking about Chaim Potok's contemporary classic, *The Chosen,* I usually start, as the book does, with the fiercely competitive baseball game between the school teams of two rival Jewish sects in Brooklyn. The game becomes nearly murderous, and Danny at the bat comes close to blinding the pitcher, Reuven. Afterwards, Danny visits Reuven in the hospital; I read from their candid, angry confrontation. A close friendship grows from the initial intensity, and Reuven becomes involved in Danny's conflict with his austere Hasidic rabbi father.

Of course this book is of direct interest if you have a big Jewish population. But that brings me to my next point in selection. I always try to integrate some books about regions and cultures *different* from those of the audience—to show the rich diversity of people and also the universal concerns we all share.

Books, particularly fiction and autobiography, can break down ethnocentricity and humanize what appears strange and foreign, so that you get to care about the individual instead of being blinded by the stereotype. And knowing the truth about the "other" individual extends your view of yourself.

One of the misleading myths perpetuated by bland popular fiction is that there is only one norm, usually as defined by the dominant white, suburban, middle-class culture. The impression is given that difference belongs with the outlandish in science fiction or fantasy, monsters that provide shivery entertainment. But reading *only* literature that perpetuates such a limited view is poor preparation for a world of cultural diversity. Separation from those who are different breeds fear and prejudice.

Except for rare special occasions (such as Black History Week or United Nations Day) or for curricular-related projects, I would not give a talk on a single ethnic group or on "World Cultures." I integrate these books in every talk I give. In each case I talk about the culture or setting or historical period, but I do not focus on it. My emphasis always is to show that the book—whatever its setting—is relevant to the lives of the young people I'm talking to.

Maxine Hong Kingston's *The Woman Warrior: Memoirs of a Girlhood among Ghosts* is a fiercely honest autobiography about growing up female and Chinese-American in California, caught by both the ghosts of Chinese tradition and the alien values of the United States.

I tell how her parents try to marry her off to one of the new immigrants, the FOBs, Fresh-off-the-Boats:

> The girls said *they'd* never date an FOB. My mother took one home from the laundry, and I saw him looking over our photographs. "This one," he said, picking up my sister's picture.
>
> "No. No," said my mother. "This one," my picture. "The oldest first," she said. Good. I was an obstacle. I would protect my sister and myself at the same time. As my parents and the FOB sat talking at the kitchen table, I dropped two dishes. I found my walking stick and limped across the floor. I twisted my mouth and caught my hand in the knots of my hair. I spilled soup on the FOB when I handed him his bowl. "She can sew, though," I heard my mother say, "and sweep." I raised dust swirls sweeping around and under the FOB's chair—very bad luck because spirits live inside the broom. I put on my shoes with the open flaps and flapped about like a Wino Ghost. From then on, I wore those shoes to parties, whenever the mothers gathered to talk about marriages. The FOB and my parents paid me no attention, half ghosts half invisible, but when he left, my mother yelled at me about the dried-duck

voice, the bad temper, the laziness, the clumsiness, the stupidity that comes from reading too much. The young men stopped visiting; not one came back. "Couldn't you just stop rubbing your nose?" she scolded. "All the village ladies are talking about your nose. They're afraid to eat our pastries because you might have kneaded the dough." But I couldn't stop at will anymore. [p. 194]

This passage makes a funny read-aloud. But add a sentence or quotation to show that the book is angry and painful. The anguish of being a stranger will touch young people everywhere, and this book fits well with any outsider theme.

As I select, besides making sure that minority and regional and world cultures are integrated, I try to have some balance of male and female protagonists. I include some exciting nonfiction.

I plan the booktalk as a whole, varying intensity and tone so that there are dramatic climaxes and moments of humor and quiet sharing. I pace the presentation so that a long dramatic scene from one book is followed by several quick talks, then perhaps a read-aloud, and so on.

I always start with a simple book of action and excitement to grab even the reluctant readers. Later I integrate more subtle and difficult titles.

I usually try to end on a note of intensity or humor, or with reconciliation after books of conflict. Poems make fine endings. But sometimes I may end without a neat conclusion, leaving things open, indicating that I could go on and on, there are so many more wonderful books . . .

TALKING ABOUT ONE BOOK

You can talk about a book in a number of ways:

> You can focus on the general plot or basic situation.
> You can focus on one particular incident or scene.
> You can focus on a character.
> You can use some combination of these.
> And with all these, you can read aloud.

General Situation

Create the world of the book as dramatically as you can. In *Finding David Dolores*, a YA novel by Margaret Willey, teenager Arly develops a crush on an older boy. She knows almost nothing about him, but she's in love. She follows David everywhere, watches him from afar, hangs around where he lives, even takes things from the garbage outside his house. She keeps her crush secret from her too-nosy mother, but she talks and talks to her friend about him, enjoying what is almost a fantasy—and then she gets to meet him.[1]

For Felice Holman's YA classic *Slake's Limbo,* I combine the writer's words with links of my own to recreate the outsider's isolation. Orphan Slake, slapped up in the morning by a kind of aunt, a scorned and tormented outsider at school and on the streets—small, nearsighted, dreaming, bruised—feels he is a worthless lump. One day, when the gangs are after him, he takes refuge in the subway. He stays there, making a home for himself, and survives underground for 121 days.

A focus on the basic plot is often the best way to talk about science fiction, where emphasis tends to be on the clever ideas about specially created worlds. In Isaac Asimov's *Fantastic Voyage,* a man has knowledge on which the fate of the world depends. He's dying of a blood clot in the brain. Four men and a woman in an atomic submarine are miniaturized and injected into the bloodstream of the dying man. They have sixty minutes to fight the patient's antibodies, pass through the heart, and try to get to the brain to destroy the clot with a laser beam.

I usually try this approach for quick talks, giving just enough of the basic conflict or dramatic situation to hook students and make them want to read on. Of course the brevity of the talk must in no way imply that the book is of lesser value.

Integrating this short intense approach with longer presentations provides variety in tone and pace and allows you to introduce more books.

Be careful that you don't give away too much of the story. You want to stimulate readers to read on for themselves.

Particular Incident

Describe the basic situation very briefly and then focus on a particular telling incident, sometimes with a brief read-aloud. This is one way I talk about Cormier's *The Chocolate War*:

Everyone at the Catholic high school Trinity is required to sell chocolates in aid of school funds. It's supposed to be voluntary, but the pressure makes it impossible to resist—except for one boy, Jerry Renault, who refuses. Brother Leon, the corrupt teacher in charge of the chocolate sale, calls the roll in the classroom each morning, asking each student how many boxes he's sold. Name by name, alphabetically, the voices shout out: "One" . . . "Five." Brother Leon gets to P. "Parmentier," he asks. "Three," Parmentier calls out. Then the teacher gets to Jerry

1. See Ilene Cooper's starred Focus review in *Booklist* (82:1023, March 1, 1986) for a discussion of how this book evokes the experience of romantic obsession.

Renault. "Renault." There's a pause. "No!" Jerry is pale, the teacher is in shock.

> It seemed almost as if Jerry and the teacher were reflections in a mirror.
> Finally Brother Leon looked down.
> "Renault," he said again, his voice like a whip.
> "No. I'm not going to sell the chocolates." [Dell ed., p. 89]

At first Jerry is a hero in the school—no one really wants to sell those chocolates, and sales begin to drop. That's when the school authorities and the brutal school gang join together to break him.[2]

Quarrels, with their flaring confrontations, make dramatic incidents for booktalks.

In Jamaica Kincaid's *Annie John,* Annie, growing up on the Caribbean island of Antigua, changes from a happy secure child to a defiant teenager. Annie and her mother used to adore each other. Now they are fighting, and their quarrels are fierce and painful. Kincaid shows the conflict between mother and daughter and the conflict inside Annie herself, and we see that Annie rebels because she feels her mother is rejecting her. After one of their wounding quarrels, in which her mother has called Annie a slut for hanging around with boys and Annie has replied, "Well . . . like mother, like daughter," Annie feels:

> I wanted to go over and put my arms around her and beg forgiveness for the thing I had just said and to explain that I didn't really mean it. But I couldn't move, and when I looked down it was as if the ground had opened up between us, making a deep and wide split. [p. 103]

Afterwards, alone in her room:

> My heart just broke, and I cried and cried. At that moment, I missed my mother more than I had ever imagined possible and wanted only to live somewhere quiet and beautiful with her alone, but also at that moment I wanted only to see her lying dead, all withered and in a coffin at my feet. [pp. 105–6]

Character

This kind of talk is especially appropriate if character is the central focus of the book.

In Cynthia Voigt's *The Runner* the interest is not so much in what hap-

---

2. I've debated whether to include this last paragraph, since it gives away quite a lot of the story. I've decided it is more important not to mislead. If I ended after the quotation, listeners might expect a story of triumph. This is a brutal book, and the talk must indicate that.

pens as in getting to know the strong, unconventional—not always likeable—hero and seeing him struggle to change.

Bullet (he named himself), seventeen years old, is strong, hard, alone; contemptuous of the weak; smart, but suspicious of books and talk; prejudiced against blacks. He runs ten miles a day, every day, and he is the Maryland state champion, but only cross-country, never on a track; in everything he is proud that "he ran himself." He is angry much of the time, fighting his cold, bullying father. But in a rage one day, he accidentally kills his sister's dog, and that shocks him into realizing how much he is becoming like his father. Bullet reaches beyond himself: in his athletics, and in his personal life, where a challenging relationship with a clever black runner helps overcome his racism. But he remains fierce and apart, determined that no one will box him in.

In Jan Slepian's *The Alfred Summer,* Lester, age fourteen, is clever, funny, and sensitive, but most people don't know it because he can barely talk. He has cerebral palsy. When the ball from the neighborhood kids bounces near him, he falls over. A boy apologizes and asks if Lester's okay. Lester is telling the story:

> Now here's the thing: I want to say, sure I'm okay, or, that's all right, I'm fine. Something like that. Well, if he has an hour or two to spare I'll get it out. I might in that time be able to tell him what's on my mind. In other words . . . in other words I have no words. Or none that I can get out without looking as if I'm strangling. At least with people I don't know. I have millions . . . billions! inside me, but if I try to say hello and you're a stranger, you have to wait awhile. A little patience, please. I can say it, you understand, but I have to choose which wires to pull to make things work and that takes time. Besides, the effort sets up the jangles. Then the old arms wave and I get all tippy toes, stepping from one foot to the other. [p. 3]

Lester feels dependent and frustrated, but he finds freedom when he helps three other outsiders in a daring project.

Reading Aloud

Sometimes the author's own words are the best lure to a book, and reading aloud can be used with all the booktalk methods.

The opening of Katherine Paterson's *The Great Gilly Hopkins* makes a superb character booktalk, as well as being an introduction to the situation and tone.

> "Gilly," said Miss Ellis with a shake of her long blond hair toward the passenger in the back seat. "I need to feel that you are willing to make some effort."
>
> Galadriel Hopkins shifted her bubble gum to the front of her mouth and

began to blow gently. She blew until she could barely see the shape of the social worker's head through the pink bubble.

"This will be your third home in less than three years." Miss Ellis swept her golden head left to right and then began to turn the wheel in a cautious maneuver to the left. "I would be the last person to say that it was all your fault. The Dixons' move to Florida, for example. Just one of those unfortunate things. And Mrs. Richmond having to go into the hospital"—it seemed to Gilly that there was a long, thoughtful pause before the caseworker went on—"for her nerves."

Pop!

Miss Ellis flinched and glanced in the rear-view mirror but continued to talk in her calm, professional voice while Gilly picked at the bits of gum stuck in her straggly bangs and on her cheeks and chin. "We should have been more alert to her condition before placing any foster child there. *I* should have been more alert." Cripes, thought Gilly. The woman was getting sincere. What a pain. "I'm not trying to *blame* you, Gilly. It's just that I need, we all need, your cooperation if any kind of arrangement is to work out." Another pause. "I can't imagine you *enjoy* all this moving around." The blue eyes in the mirror were checking out Gilly's response. "Now this new foster mother is very different from Mrs. Nevins." Gilly calmly pinched a blob of gum off the end of her nose. There was no use trying to get the gum out of her hair. [p. 1]

Why touch anything so good? Read it.

When you read aloud:

Do it only if the author's style is good—otherwise you may be better off telling it in your own words. Read aloud when you want to communicate the individual author's voice or the drama of a confrontation.

Keep it short. The previous quotation from Paterson is one of the longest I use. Sometimes one or two sentences are enough.

In Lynn Hall's *Just One Friend*, Dory is sensitive and strong, but she is mentally slow. She tells her own story: "One of the worst things about being dumb in a regular school is that the other kids get the idea that you don't have any feelings . . . [p. 22]." The booktalk doesn't need any more than that. Just add a sentence to say that Dory's desperate attempt to find a friend leads to a tragic accident.[3]

Know the passage very well so that you can look up often and not lose eye contact with your audience while you're reading.

Have your markers clearly in place—and even mark passages in pencil—so that your presentation is smooth.

Edit a little if you have to. Cut out references that aren't relevant to the

---

3. See Stephanie Zvirin's starred review in *Booklist* (82:124, September 15, 1985) for insight into the book's sensitivity and power.

scene you're reading. Shorten sometimes. Make sure that every word counts.

But don't edit out the author's style. Remember, that's why you've chosen to read aloud, because this writer says it much better than you can paraphrase.

Don't edit out the difficult words or allusions. I leave in the word *temerity* in the quotation from *Oliver Twist* in chapter 1. One of the important side benefits of reading aloud is that it communicates the reading level, so that listeners can tell whether they can handle reading it on their own. I learned a lesson when I booktalked *Great Expectations*—the terrifying opening with the convict rising up at Pip from the graveyard; crazy Miss Havisham who stopped the clocks when she was jilted on her wedding day; and her ward Estella, whom Pip loves but who's been raised to get revenge on men—I did a great job with the story and the atmosphere. But then afterwards a girl who couldn't possibly handle the reading level rushed to check out the book and I was ashamed I'd misled her. Now when I talk about *Great Expectations,* I also read aloud enough to communicate Dickens's vocabulary and style.

Even if you don't read aloud, *steep yourself in the world of the book.* As you prepare, reread parts of the book to absorb the atmosphere, the telling detail.

In survival stories, the detail is crucial. Whenever I booktalk Jack London, I reread a chapter or story to feel again the savage, desolate landscape. His animals are fierce and hungry, and often there's a solitary human fighting for survival. I keep notes of the exact temperature, the number of remaining cartridges, the number of wolves and how close they are.

Choosing the Situation, Incident, or Character

Here we get back to the basic approach: Choose what gives you pleasure, what you want to share with others, the scene or situation that stays with you. You have to trust that response in yourself. That comes first.

Of course there may be times when the scene or situation you love most may not be the best way to communicate the book to others—especially when the episode requires a great deal of explanation or introduction. You may have to try another way into the book.

It took me a few attempts before I found an effective way to draw readers into Walter Tevis's hypnotic novel, *The Queen's Gambit,* about the world of championship chess and a young girl's drive to the top. I learned not to talk much about the chess (except to the chess club), but to focus on the bleak orphan nobody who is really a genius.

Marion Carter of Salt Lake City Public Library showed me that the best way into Peck's *A Day No Pigs Would Die* is not with the focus on the Shakers (as I was trying to do) but with the dramatic first chapter: the outsider boy who's run away from the teasing at school; the calf he helps get born; and the reward he receives from the grateful farmer—a tiny pig, the boy's first pet.[4]

Bobbie Ann Mason's *In Country* is an adult novel about contemporary Kentucky teenager Samantha, who is concerned about the war in Vietnam:

> It was the summer of the Michael Jackson *Victory* tour and the Bruce Springsteen *Born in the U.S.A.* tour, neither of which Sam got to go to. At her graduation, the commencement speaker, a Methodist minister, had preached about keeping the country strong, stressing sacrifice. He made Sam nervous. She started thinking about war, and it stayed on her mind all summer. [p. 23]

That read-aloud immediately communicates the book's accessible style and familiar setting. I explain that Sam's father died in Vietnam before she was born. As she hangs around the shopping malls and has her girlfriend pierce her ears for a second set of earrings and watches M*A*S*H reruns with her uncle and her boyfriend, she tries to find out about the war and about her father. Out running one day, she asks Tom, a young veteran, if he knows where Quang Ngai is:

> "My daddy died over there right before I was born, but everybody acts like it's a big secret. I don't know much about him."
> "A lot of boys just plain got forgotten," Tom said. "And a lot of the ones who came back feel guilty that they're the ones who made it back."
> "Do you feel that way?"
> "Sure."
> "Did you think you were doing the right thing over there?"
> "I didn't know what I was doing," he said. [p. 77]

In the chapter on war, I booktalk this novel somewhat differently, though the essential elements are there—the immediate contemporary scene, Sam's search for her father, and her struggle to find meaning in the war. You might very well choose differently. There are dozens of accessible scenes and incidents. For example, if you're talking about family

---

4. This informal booktalk exchange occurred at a dynamic preconference on booktalking organized by the Young Adult Services Division of ALA in 1982, where booktalkers discussed their techniques in small, hands-on workshops. I came back with dozens of new ideas.

themes, you might use the candid scene where Sam tries to find out if her mother loved Sam's father.[5]

I generally choose something

that delights me
that is central to the book's theme or story
that is inherently dramatic
that doesn't require much introduction.

USING THEMES

Finding a Theme

Finding a theme is easy if you keep the connections very loose and remember that it's the books you're promoting, not the theme. You may start with the books or with the theme or with some interaction between them.

Start with the books you want to talk about and you'll see that patterns emerge, that the books fall into groups. I often start with a core of books and then look for ways of putting them together. I add some, drop some, choose more. I bring in books for intensity, some for variety. I make a special dynamic book a climactic point.

Consider giving a talk on this year's Best Books for Young Adults list. You have certain favorites that you *must* talk about. Some of them connect with each other and lead you to others on the list. Then you realize that you need to integrate more science fiction, or that you need to balance male and female protagonists better. That changes things around a little. You choose something dramatic to start with; one or two to read aloud; several to mention briefly; a few to discuss at length. My "Booktalking Them off the Shelves" articles in *School Library Journal,* August 1984 and April 1986, discuss booktalking the year's best books in a thematic way; there are dozens of possible combinations.

Or start with a theme that is broad-ranging and intense, such as terror. You can integrate terror in the wilderness, in the family, in war, in school, in love, within the self. The same applies to themes such as survival or the outsider. Or you can use subjects, such as animals or sports.

Take terror.

---

5. For another view of this book and its relevance to young adults, read Roger Sutton's column, "In the YA Corner," in *School Library Journal* (32:86, January 1986). I heard Linda Waddle, librarian at Cedar Falls High School, Iowa, booktalk *In Country* by focusing on Sam's nurturing relationship with her uncle Emmett.

I always start a booktalk with a highly dramatic story, full of action. Gillian Cross's *On the Edge* is a thriller with physical and psychological terror.

Tug has been out running. As he comes back to his London house and unlocks the front door, he feels uneasy: "Dark! The house was too dark . . . . And there was something else . . . ." He stretches out his hand towards the light switch—

> Then everything crashed round him. No light. Instead, from behind, from the other side of the door, a body launched itself. An arm went chokingly round his neck and a hand pressed against his face, forcing a pad over his nostrils. [p. 6]

Tug's kidnappers try to brainwash him, and they beat him up. (See the chapter on terror for a longer talk on this book.)

From there you can move to child-abuse books, such as Bette Greene's *Summer of My German Soldier,* and to terror in the family, such as Suzanne Newton's *I Will Call It Georgie's Blues.* Or you can move from the brainwashing in *On the Edge* to George Orwell's *1984.* If you want to lighten the tone, you can move to Douglas Adams's science-fiction comedy *The Hitchhiker's Guide to the Galaxy,* in which Earth has been demolished to make way for an intergalactic speedway, and Englishman Arthur Dent wakes up to find himself hitching with an alien on a starship. Or there's the delicious, shivery terror of Barbara Michaels's adult thriller, *Be Buried in the Rain,* with its mixture of family secrets, mystery, and romance. There's terror in war. Then nuclear war.

But you've also got to think of those readers who don't want so much physical action. Bring in emotional stories of personal conflict, such as Paula Fox's haunting young adult novel *The Moonlight Man,* about a girl who discovers that the father she's always romanticized is intelligent and charming but also a desperate alcoholic.

Whatever the theme, the booktalk should range widely to appeal to a variety of readers. A talk on sports may start with games and physical action, but it must also bring in sports books about inner struggle (such as Robert Lipsyte's *The Contender*), fantasy and love (such as Nancy Willard's *Things Invisible to See*), nonfiction (David Halberstam's *The Amateurs*), and mystery (Rosemary Wells's *When No One Was Looking*). A talk on love may integrate action, adventure, family stories, and perhaps animal stories as well as romance and passion.

Chapter 4 shows in detail how a talk on war, like the one on terror, may include exciting stories of heroic adventure, but also war in the family, between lovers, in space, at school, within one person.

Loosen the theme to cover a sequence of subjects. You don't need to keep rigidly to the same theme throughout the talk. You can loosen the theme considerably as you go along, perhaps move into another theme, and then another. You might start off by talking about various animal stories, including *The Incredible Journey*. Then you can use the journey link to talk about Voigt's *Homecoming* (in which a family of kids abandoned by their mother walk to find a relative to take them in). That homelessness connects to *Slake's Limbo* (in which a boy makes a home in the subway). That can lead into fantasy about underground kingdoms . . . and so on.

On the other hand, as long as the theme is loose and broad and allows you to introduce all kinds of books, you may want to keep to one organizing theme and use a variety of quiet links and transitions.

Remember, the emphasis is on the books, not the theme.

Connecting the Books

I use all kinds of links between books to connect them in a smooth, informal way. For example:

Common objects or situations. A mysterious house can link the romantic suspense of *Rebecca* and the YA historical fiction *Ask Me No Questions.* A mouse can link the science fiction *Flowers for Algernon* (in which brain experiments are performed on the mouse Algernon before they are tried on the human subject Charlie); the Holocaust survival story *The Island on Bird Street* (in which a mouse is the boy's only companion); and the macabre and funny autobiographical stories in *Boy* (where the young Roald Dahl uses a dead mouse to wreak revenge on the mean sweetshop lady).

Setting. The north of England links books as diverse as *Wuthering Heights*; Howker's YA short stories, *Badger on the Barge*; and Herriot's cheery, affectionate memoirs of his life as a veterinarian. A school setting links the *The Chocolate War, A Separate Peace,* and *Remembering the Good Times.*

Relationships. Sisters link *A Summer to Die* by Lois Lowry with Katherine Paterson's *Jacob Have I Loved,* about a girl jealous of her talented twin. And both can link to the brothers in S. E. Hinton's *Tex.* You can do the same with fathers, grandparents, etc.

Genre. Biography or fantasy or drama can link books on the most diverse subjects. You can move from the life of a sports star to the biography of a musician or a war survivor. You can connect Robin McKinley's splendid fantasy, *The Hero and the Crown* (in which Aerin, an outsider in her father's kingdom, fights Maur, the Black Dragon) with the very different fantasy hero in Clare Bell's *Ratha's Creature* (in which an intelligent wild cat, living millions of years ago, discovers fire). You can tell a short story and use it as a link to an anthology or a writer or a theme.[6]

Author. An author can lead from one subject to another. Through the author Bruce Brooks you can link basketball in *The Moves Make the Man* to classical music or fatherhood or the decade of the sixties in his *Midnight Hour Encores.*

An intense word or image. The word *secrets* can be a great lure, linking *Jane Eyre, Sirens and Spies,* and a host of other books.[7] Anne Frank says she feels like a caged bird when she describes her feelings of claustrophobia and depression in hiding:[8] this provides a clear link from Holocaust racism to Maya Angelou's *I Know Why the Caged Bird Sings,* about growing up in the racist Depression South.

Contrast. You can use the same kind of links in contrast. I move from the bleak home of *Slake's Limbo* to the cozy togetherness of Mildred Taylor's *Roll of Thunder, Hear My Cry,* in which the strong black family stands together against Klan violence. I contrast the shut-in terror of a prison or of the mental ward in *One Flew over the Cuckoo's Nest* with the young wife's terror in the wide wilderness of *Prairie Songs.*

To move from action and science fiction to stories of inner struggle, I might say "Sometimes a book about the terror inside one person can be as intense as global warfare;" or "Sometimes the space between two people can be as wide as the wilderness."

Poetry and Theme

Poetry is an excellent way to link books. A poem can bring in contrast or intensify your theme.

And theme is a natural way to make poetry accessible. With a quiet connection you can introduce a poet or an anthology, or one poem alone, or just one line, apt and echoing.

Use poetry sparingly. Keep your reading direct, immediate, and brief. Choose something that is relevant to today's young people and that lures them with sound and rhythm and with focused imagery and wordplay.

As always, choose what you love, what stays with you. In her introduction to her YA collection of love poems, *Love Lines,* Betsy Hearne talks

6. See Brad Hooper's international bibliography of classic short-story writers, "Tried and True: Old Masters of the Short Story," in the Adults Section of *Booklist* (83:689–90, January 1, 1987). It includes writers from Ambrose Bierce and Willa Cather to D. H. Lawrence, Guy de Maupassant, and Mark Twain.

7. Roger Sutton first made me aware of this "secrets" hook. I use it all the time.

8. Anne Frank, *The Diary of a Young Girl,* entry for Friday, October 29, 1943 (Doubleday, 1952; Pocket Edition, 1953, p. 102).

about enjoying poetry: "A few lines a day will keep you company . . . .
Like love, poetry takes time. . . . Poems consumed in gulps are boring,
even numbing. But if they're sipped, the lines slip into your mind to fit the
feelings whenever they come back."

A simple strong poem can introduce an anthology. After books about
savage conflict, I might vary the tone with what I call my favorite poem of
opposition, "Song against Broccoli" by Roy Blount, Jr.:

> The local groceries are all out of broccoli,
> Loccoli.

That poem is anthologized in Paul Janeczko's *Pocket Poems,* and reading
the poem is a good way to introduce Janeczko's lively contemporary
anthologies for young people.

With books about outsiders or terror I sometimes use the poem "'Don't
touch me!' I scream at passersby" by the Russian Natalya Gor-
banyevskaya, in *Love Is like the Lion's Tooth,* a YA anthology, edited by
Frances McCullough, of poems from all over the world that deal with
some form of passion.

Integrate a country or an ethnic or cultural tradition with a poem from
Zero Makes Me Hungry, a multi-ethnic anthology of twentieth-century
poems compiled by Edward Lueders and Primus St. John.

For Halloween read from Myra Cohn Livingston's *Why Am I Grown So
Cold?* which includes fears, nightmares, spells, omens, curses, monsters,
ghosts, and fiends in poetry from many times and places.

Use poems in translation, such as *The Yellow Canary Whose Eye Is So
Black,* edited and translated by Cheli Durán, a spaciously printed bilingual
collection of more than forty poems written in Spanish by Latin-
Americans. Read from the clear, polished poems translated from the
Japanese in the anthology *From the Country of Eight Islands.*

Read Dennis Brutus's fierce and tender poems about South Africa and
apartheid, such as "Somehow We Survive," in a collection of his work or
in one of the anthologies of African poetry—traditional and modern—
such as *Poems of Black Africa,* edited by Wole Soyinka.

Read from the fresh, modern anthologies, *Reflections on a Gift of Watermelon Pickle* and *Some Haystacks Don't Even Have Any Needle,* compiled by
Stephen Dunning and others, where one poem can hook readers to
browse through the collection.

Or use a poem by a contemporary American or British writer, such as
Marge Piercy, Ted Hughes, Denise Levertov, Paul Zimmer, Mary Oliver,
Adrienne Rich, to introduce the poet's work.

Use popular song. Try the Beatles' lyric "She's Leaving Home" with
books about family conflict. Introduce the anthology *Rock Voices: The Best*

Lyrics of an Era, edited by Matt Damsker, which includes lyrics by Bob Dylan, Laura Nyro, Paul Simon, the Beatles, Bruce Springsteen, and others. Tell students about the song "Wuthering Heights" by British pop star Kate Bush (and recorded also by Pat Benatar), with Cathy's ghost calling to Heathcliff on the moor.[9] Use folk songs and ballads: Read from "Frankie and Johnny" with themes of love. I read my favorite stanza:

> With the first shot Johnny staggered;
>   with the second shot he fell;
> When the third bullet hit him,
>   there was a new man's face in hell.
> He was her man, but he done her wrong.

After a book about a journey or quest, I might read from one of the poems in the adult anthology *American Classic: Car Poems for Collectors.* Some of the poems by e. e. cummings, Karl Shapiro, and several contemporary poets evoke the power, exhilaration, and thrilling danger of driving. Some describe the machine's destructive potential; for example, William Stafford's quiet "Traveling through the Dark" relates the common driving experience of finding a wild animal run over on the road.

I often use Arnold Adoff's anthologies of black poetry, especially *I Am the Darker Brother,* available as a small, spaciously printed, accessible paperback. It includes Langston Hughes, who is one of the best poets for reading aloud: direct, rhythmic, wry, intense. I read his "Me and the Mule" or the heartbreaking "Song for a Dark Girl." Robert Hayden also speaks powerfully to young people: I read the section on Harriet Tubman in his "Runagate Runagate"; in talks on family conflict I use his "Those Winter Sundays" about his father, or I use Gwendolyn Brooks's "A Song in the Front Yard" about a child in a secure, happy home longing for adventure.

It is important to use poetry that has images and concerns relevant to contemporary teenage experience. But relevant does not only mean contemporary. Read from Blake's "The Tyger" ("Tyger! Tyger! burning bright") or from his deceptively simple "London":

> I wander thro' each charter'd street,
> Near where the charter'd Thames does flow,
> And mark in every face I meet
> Marks of weakness, marks of woe.
>   —*Songs of Experience*

---

9. My thanks to *Booklist* editorial assistant Karen Moody, who first told me about this song, and that it made her read the book.

Don't neglect the elemental appeal of sound and rhythm. From my childhood I remember hearing my father in the shower belting out lines and lines of Hamlet's soliloquies or Tennyson's "Charge of the Light Brigade" or Sir Walter Scott's bombast:

> Breathes there the man with soul so dead
> Who never to himself hath said
> This is my own, my native land . . .
> —from "The Lay of the Last Minstrel," 1805

Most of the poetry had little meaning for me, but I caught his love of the words, and the recitations still sing in my mind. And from that time I still have lines such as the first stanza from Christina Rossetti's exquisite nineteenth-century lyric, which will move today's young people as it moves me and my father:

> Song
> When I am dead, my dearest,
> Sing no sad songs for me;
> Plant thou no roses at my head,
> Nor shady cypress tree:
> Be the green grass above me
> With showers and dewdrops wet;
> And if thou wilt, remember,
> And if thou wilt, forget.

PRACTICAL BASICS

Getting into the Classroom

Booktalking in the library at lunchtime or after school is a valuable literary and social activity, but you'll only get the eager readers. As much as possible, I booktalk in the classroom as part of class time so that I reach some students who aren't reading.

Show faculty and administration that booktalking can generate enthusiasm for reading and that it can promote good books. Mike Printz, librarian at Topeka West High School, Kansas, gives an annual booktalk to faculty during planning week before school begins in the fall. He speaks about books teachers might enjoy and discusses what kids are reading. Ask to speak at department meetings. Tell the English department about quality YA literature and show them that you care about good books as they do. I worked with some English teachers who knew the best YA literature and respected it, and who taught me how to find the myth of the hero and the perilous journey in contemporary books. Social studies teachers used literature to humanize history[10] and stimulated rich social studies/English/library cooperation.

Prepare bibliographies (always annotated) or, if you don't have time to do them yourself, use those that appear regularly in *Booklist* (on everything from Growing Up Hispanic to World Cultures to Whodunits) and sometimes in other journals (for example, Eugene LaFaille's science fiction list in VOYA on nuclear war will interest many YA readers.)[11] Use the *Booklist* contemporary classics bibliographies, prepared by the YA and children's editors, available in attractive brochures.[12] Send the lists to teachers who might be interested, and offer to come and talk to classes about some of the books.

Always include some books that will push students beyond themselves. Teachers won't ask you back if you give students only what they can find on their own.

I insist that the teacher stay all the time so that I don't have to worry about discipline. It's very hard to be a stranger in somebody else's classroom unless you come as an honored guest. Mary K. Chelton warns against being used as a substitute teacher: "Classes are notorious for going berserk when they think an inexperienced substitute is on the scene, and teachers who have never had booktalkers before are equally notorious for disappearing the whole period."[13]

Booktalking Styles

As I have outlined above, and as the following chapters will show, my favorite booktalking style is some combination of telling and reading. But that may not be your style at all. And I certainly don't read aloud with every book. (In some of the best books the parts may be so unified that it is difficult to find a passage that can stand alone without long explanations. Or you may need to telescope many elements together.) Use the style that suits you and that fits each book best.

Prevent burnout by always trying at least one new book, by using an

10. See *Booklist*'s multimedia bibliographies, prepared by the YA and non-print editors, on such topics as "Humanizing History" (82:973, March 1, 1986), and "World Cultures: Beyond Our Shores" (82:1408, May 15, 1986).

11. Eugene LaFaille, "Nuclear War: Visions of the Apocalypse in Books and Films," *VOYA* 9:15 (April 1986).

12. "Books for Everychild" (September 1, 1983); "Information for Everychild" (July 1985); "Junior High Contemporary Classics" (December 15, 1984); "Contemporary Classics for Young Adults" (July, 1985); "Contemporary Nonfiction for Young Adults" (January 1, 1986).

13. Mary K. Chelton, "Booktalking—You Can Do It," *School Library Journal*, 22:39–43 (April 1976).

old book in a new way, or by experimenting with new themes and genres.

Talk with other booktalkers. Learn from them what approaches they use for particular titles, what scene or incident moves a book off the shelf (as I described with *A Day No Pigs Would Die*). *Booklist* YA editor Sally Estes speaks with such authority and joy about science fiction and fantasy that she has persuaded me to read a whole range of great titles I might have missed. Try to meet with other booktalkers in your district or system. Come to the Booktalking Discussion Group that meets regularly at ALA conferences.

In her fine introductory chapters to *Booktalk! 2*, Joni Bodart discusses in detail the pros and cons of various booktalking styles; and the hands-on chapters by Elizabeth Overmyer on "Booktalking for Children" and by Larry Rakow on "Booktalking from the School Librarian's Perspective" are both inspiring and practical. This anthology of Joni's and other people's booktalks includes a great variety of excellent examples.[14]

In preparing for the presentation, some experienced booktalkers write it all out and learn the talk by heart. Until I had to get down examples for this book, I never wrote out a talk (though I kept notes on important details—names, settings, read-aloud passages, etc.). I find that writing and memorizing reduces the sense of excitement and spontaneity for me. It also takes a long time and limits me to too few books. And why memorize if you can read aloud?

The point about personal style also applies to how you present the books. You may like to interact with the audience as you go along. You may prefer to leave time at the end for discussion with the group and with individual students. I usually prefer the latter, a structured talk with discussion at the end, so that concentration isn't broken. (To be honest, most people, including young adults, don't booktalk very well without preparation: you don't want someone in the class launching into an unprepared, rambling plot summary of a related title.) But you may prefer a less formal approach. In any case, be prepared for enthusiastic interruption, positive or negative; and be flexible enough to drop a title quickly if the group isn't interested or if many of them already know the book well.

Some people use audiovisual aids. I find them distracting. Even an overhead projector means that the lights have to be out and I lose eye contact with my audience. But I do talk about the visual. Even though the

---

14. Joni Bodart, *Booktalk! 2: Booktalking for All Ages and Audiences* (Wilson, 1985). Joni was the first to write books about booktalking. Her *Booktalk!* (1980) and *Booktalk! 2*, together with her column in *VOYA*, have played an essential role in promoting booktalking.

class can't see the pictures close up, I describe them briefly in context and suggest students come up and look at the books for themselves after the talk. David Macaulay's *Castle* fits well with themes of war; his *Underground* (with text and drawings depicting the foundations, transport, and support systems that run under a city) has wide appeal for all ages. The large-size Pennyroyal edition of *Frankenstein* with Barry Moser's terrifying woodcuts showing the giant demon against lonely land and seascapes is a fine introduction to the classic outsider story. I also use photographs, such as Timothy Ferris's *Spaceshots: the Beauty of Nature beyond Earth* or South African photojournalist Peter Magubane's searing pictures of apartheid in *Black Child*. The period photographs in Russell Freedman's *Immigrant Kids* and *Children of the Wild West* draw young people to the books and their historical subjects.

Whatever style you use, you must prepare very carefully. Have your books ready in the order you will talk about them, with markers in place for read-aloud passages. Know those passages very well. Practice what you will say about each book and how you will link books. If you fumble around a lot, you'll lose you listeners' attention.

Some Don'ts and Qualifications

The basic don't is never to give away the story. Leave your listeners wanting to read on for themselves, wanting to know more of the story, the characters and their world, or the ideas.

Reading is essentially a private experience. You don't want to get between the reader and the book. I said earlier that you should steep yourself in the book's details. The warning is, don't overdo it, especially if the book doesn't need it. There's a delicate balance in booktalking. Say just enough to entice the young person to the book, and then leave reader and book alone together. John Donovan, executive director of the Children's Book Council and a fine YA author, made me sharply aware of the danger of being intrusive and overbearing. In his acceptance speech of the Chicago Children's Reading Round Table 1983 Award, he said:

> The reading experience is between the person who wrote the book and the person who chooses to read it. If a lot of people read a book, the author may have connected; if few people read a book, but are affected by it in a way that remains with them, the author of that book has also connected. Connections are what is important in communicating with young people. The rest of us— the communications industry, including publishers, producers, reviewers, teachers, librarians, etc.—are just intermediaries: we either facilitate or obstruct.

Many superb books can be talked about very simply. There's often no need for a long booktalk. Susan Cooper's fantasy series, *The Dark Is Rising,* is read over and over again by fans from fifth graders through adults. To hook readers into these books, I briefly introduce one of them, using a scene where the young people confront the powerful forces of the Dark. With some books you don't need much more than a title: *The Changeover: A Supernatural Romance.* Or an author: Judy Blume.

Roger Sutton says that all he needs to say about Richard Peck's *Are You in the House Alone?* is "There's this babysitter . . . ."

The sinister opening situation is a perfect and simple introduction to Shirley Jackson's classic thriller, *We Have Always Lived in the Castle.* Merricat Blackwood lives alone with her sister Constance and her Uncle Julian. Everyone else in the family is dead, poisoned by a fatal dose of arsenic in the sugar bowl. Or just read the chilling opening paragraph.

Such brief booktalks are what librarians use all the time in readers' advisory work at the desk or on the floor.

As much as possible, keep yourself out of the way. You want your audience to remember the book—and that you liked it—not your charismatic performance. As Mary K. Chelton says, if you are "so entertaining that only your dramatic ability dazzles your audience, you may be missing the point."[15]

But you don't want to be anonymous. Keep your energy level high. Speak with enthusiasm; communicate that you care about the characters. When you lose that passion about a book, it's time to stop talking about it, at least for a while.

Keep it as uncluttered as possible. Your talk is not a plot summary. For the talk on *The Chocolate War* in this chapter, I decided that I didn't need to tell about Jerry's being new or a freshman, nor did I need to describe the whole Vigils gang operation. I just wanted the elemental situation—one person against the system—and a closely focused scene that dramatized the confrontation.

A booktalk is not a review. The two may start off the same; the booktalk technique of plunging into the world of the story may also make an effective opening for a book review. For example: "Nick's father is mentally ill, but he won't seek help" (*The Keeper*); or "Where was he? Where was her father?" (*The Moonlight Man*). But literary criticism doesn't belong in a booktalk.

Don't explain or analyze. In *The Chocolate War,* don't get into long discussions about power. The first time I booktalked Robert Silverberg's science fiction story "Caught in the Organ Draft," I was so excited by the layers of meaning that I discussed the symbols instead of outlining the basic situation and leaving the fine story to speak for itself.

Don't falsify, don't mislead or oversell. Don't present Zibby Oneal's sophisticated *In Summer Light* as if it were a YA romance. If you misrepresent a book, your listeners may check it out, but they won't trust you next time. And you'll have made reading a disappointing experience. Choose a passage to read aloud or discuss that is representative of the book as a whole. If it isn't true to the whole book—and sometimes with a complicated book one scene can't be representative—then you owe it to your listeners to tell them something about other crucial aspects, even if sometimes it means giving away more of the story than you'd like to. Clayton Bess's *Tracks* starts off as an action-packed adventure story about young Blue and his older brother riding the trains in the Depression; but Blue loses his innocence after he witnesses a brutal racist murder—and your talk must focus on the adventure and also warn of the horror.

If there's controversial material, mention it. Don't avoid the child abuse in *Summer of My German Soldier*, the homosexuality in *The Man without a Face*. It will help young people to hear you discuss the lesbian love story *Annie on My Mind* with other love stories. A booktalk is an excellent way to tell a group about fiction and nonfiction on subjects such as mental illness, AIDS, and teenage pregnancy in an accepting, nonjudgmental, and noninvasive way.

But don't exploit. In *I Know Why the Caged Bird Sings,* Maya Angelou describes how at eight years old she was raped by her mother's boyfriend, and how after the man was killed, in her shame and guilt she stopped talking. The booktalk must mention this. But it must also focus, as Angelou does, on how she found pride in herself with the help of her strong, loving family. I talk about those who helped her to speak again— her adored brother, Bailey; or Mrs. Flowers, "who made me proud to be Negro," and who read to Maya from Dickens and other great writers and showed her the power and beauty of the human voice.

Booktalk the Holocaust quietly. Don't wallow in the gruesome detail. When I talk about Sara Nomberg-Pryztyk's memoir, *Auschwitz,* I give the facts of the camps; I warn of the horror of nightmare realized; sometimes I tell one of the stark vignettes. I include something of the Holocaust in almost every booktalk—the material is elemental and gripping; young people want to know about it; and it is important that they know—but I am careful that the booktalk neither exploits the horror nor offers slick comfort. I try to move from the emotion to some kind of moral inquiry, as in Myron Levoy's *Alan and Naomi,* where a Jewish-American boy tries to cope with the overwhelming evil.

One last don't. Don't expect to please all young people all the time, however popular your booktalks. The seventh grader who seeks you out daily to talk about Lloyd Alexander may avoid you in high school. The reverse is also true, of course: suddenly the sophomore whose reading seems to have been limited to the daily horoscope finds the library. And years later someone you barely remember may come up to you: "You know that book you told me about . . . ."

Don't be discouraged if they act bored while you're talking. Or if they don't want to check out the books in the classroom. Usually in junior high they will storm the truck at the end of the talk, and that's a wonderful response. But sometimes, especially with the older students, the important thing may be to act cool with their peers. Give students space. Even if they want a book very badly—sometimes especially if they're deeply moved by hearing about the book, or if the subject is controversial—they may want to check out the book when they are alone. So I sometimes say that I will leave the booktruck in a particular place in the library where they can come and check out the books at their leisure.

From Booktalking to the Library

I always connect the booktalk to the library. I tell the class where in the library they can find the books I've discussed and others like them. I ask for the students' suggestions and take them seriously. If a book they want is already taken, I promise to let them know when it comes in, and I keep that promise, sending a brief note. This is individualized attention: it matters to me that that student gets that book.

When I booktalk, students get to know me. It makes them feel welcome in the library. In talking to them about books, I have been sharing feelings and ideas, talking about what moves me, what is exciting to me. I've shown them what I care about.

When they like the books, they come to the library for more. They trust my recommendations and give me theirs. They may share their enthusiasm about the books with me—tersely ("The ending was so *sad*") or ebulliently ("I stayed up reading until 4 A.M."), or they may not want to talk at all. The books are a bond between us.

BOOKS DISCUSSED

Adams, Douglas. *The Hitchhiker's Guide to the Galaxy*. Harmony, 1980. Adult; gr. 8 up

American Classic: Car Poems for Collectors. Ed. by Mary Swope. SCOP Publications, 1986. Adult; gr. 8 up

Angelou, Maya. *I Know Why the Caged Bird Sings*. Random, 1970. Adult; gr. 8 up

Asimov, Isaac. *Fantastic Voyage*. Bantam, 1966. Adult; gr. 7 up

Bell, Clare. *Ratha's Creature*. Atheneum/Margaret K. McElderry, 1983. YA; gr. 7 up

Bess, Clayton. *Tracks*. Houghton, 1986. YA/CH; gr. 6–10

Blake, William. *Songs of Experience*. 1794. Adult; gr. 4 up

———. *Songs of Innocence*. 1789. Adult; gr. 4 up

Brontë, Charlotte. *Jane Eyre*. 1847. Adult classic; gr. 7 up

Brontë, Emily. *Wuthering Heights*. 1847. Adult classic; gr. 9 up

Brooks, Bruce. *Midnight Hour Encores*. Harper, 1986. YA; gr. 7–12

———. *The Moves Make the Man*. Harper, 1984. YA; gr. 8 up

Brutus, Dennis. *A Simple Lust*. Heinemann Ed. Books, 1973. (African Writers Series). Adult; gr. 8 up

Burnford, Sheila. *The Incredible Journey*. Little, Brown, 1961. Adult; gr. 5 up

Conrad, Pam. *Prairie Songs*. Harper, 1985. CH/YA; 6–12

Cooper, Susan. *The Dark Is Rising*. Atheneum/Margaret K. McElderry, 1973. CH/YA; gr. 5 up

Cormier, Robert. *The Chocolate War*. Pantheon, 1974. Dell, 1975. YA; gr. 7 up

Cross, Gillian. *On the Edge*. Holiday House, 1985. CH/YA; gr. 7–10

Dahl, Roald. *Boy: Tales of Childhood*. Farrar, 1984. CH/YA; gr. 5 up

Dickens, Charles. *Great Expectations*. 1861. Adult classic; gr. 8 up

Du Maurier, Daphne. *Rebecca*. Doubleday, 1938. Adult; gr. 7 up

Ferris, Timothy. *Spaceshots: The Beauty of Nature Beyond Earth*. Pantheon, 1985. Adult; gr. 7 up

Fox, Paula. *The Moonlight Man*. Bradbury, 1986. YA; gr. 7 up

Frank, Anne. *The Diary of a Young Girl*. Tr. from Dutch by B. M. Mooyaart. Doubleday, 1952. Adult; gr. 5 up

"Frankie and Johnny." Anon. Adult; gr. 5 up

Freedman, Russell. *Immigrant Kids*. Dutton, 1980. CH/YA; gr. 5–9

———. *Children of the Wild West*. Clarion, 1983. CH/YA; gr. 5–9

From the Country of Eight Islands: An Anthology of Japanese Poetry. Ed. and tr. by Hiroaki Sato and Burton Watson. Univ. of Washington Pr., 1981. Adult; gr. 9 up

Garden, Nancy. *Annie on My Mind*. Farrar, 1982. YA; gr. 8–12

Greene, Bette. *Summer of My German Soldier*. Dial, 1973. CH/YA; gr. 6–10

Halberstam, David. *The Amateurs*. Morrow, 1985. Adult; gr. 9 up

Hall, Lynn. *Just One Friend*. Scribner's, 1985. YA; gr. 7–10

Hearne, Betsy. *Love Lines: Poetry in Person*. Margaret K. McElderry Books, 1987. YA; gr. 8 up

Herriot, James. *All Creatures Great and Small*. St. Martin's, 1972. Adult; gr. 7 up

Hinton, S. E. *Tex*. Delacorte, 1979. YA; gr. 6–10

Holland, Isabelle. *The Man without a Face*. Lippincott, 1972. YA; gr. 7–12

Holman, Felice. *Slake's Limbo*. Scribner, 1974. CH/YA; gr. 5 up

Howker, Janni. *Badger on the Barge and Other Stories*. Greenwillow, 1985. YA; gr. 6 up

I Am the Darker Brother: An Anthology of Modern Poems by Black Americans. Ed. by Arnold Adoff. Macmillan, 1968. Collier, 1970. Adult; gr. 6 up

Jackson, Shirley. *We Have Always Lived in the Castle*. Viking, 1962. Adult; gr. 8 up.

Kesey, Ken. *One Flew over the Cuckoo's Nest*. Viking, 1962. Adult; gr. 10 up

Keyes, Daniel. *Flowers for Algernon*. Harcourt, 1966. Adult; gr. 8 up

Kincaid, Jamaica. *Annie John*. Farrar, 1985. Adult; gr. 9 up

Kingston, Maxine Hong. *The Woman Warrior: Memoirs of a Girlhood among Ghosts*. Knopf, 1977. Adult; gr. 9 up

Knowles, John. *A Separate Peace*. Macmillan, 1960. Adult; gr. 9 up

Levoy, Myron. *Alan and Naomi*. Harper, 1977. CH/YA; gr. 6–10

Lipsyte, Robert. *The Contender*. Harper, 1967. YA; gr. 7–10

Lisle, Janet Taylor. *Sirens and Spies*. Bradbury, 1985. CH/YA; gr. 7–10

Love Is Like the Lion's Tooth: An Anthology of Love Poems. Ed. by Frances McCullough. Harper, 1984. YA; gr. 7 up

Lowry, Lois. *A Summer to Die*. Houghton, 1977. CH/YA; gr. 6–10

Macaulay, David. *Castle*. Houghton, 1977. CH/YA; gr. 5 up

_____. *Underground*. Houghton, 1976. CH/YA; gr. 5 up

McKinley, Robin. *The Hero and the Crown*. Greenwillow, 1985. CH/YA; gr. 7–12

Magubane, Peter. *Black Child*. Knopf, 1982. Adult; gr. 6 up

Mahy, Margaret. *The Changeover: A Supernatural Romance*. Atheneum/Margaret K. McElderry, 1984. CH/YA; gr. 6–10

Mason, Bobbie Ann. *In Country*. Harper, 1985. Adult; gr. 8 up

Michaels, Barbara. *Be Buried in the Rain*. Atheneum, 1985. Adult; gr. 8 up

Naylor, Phyllis Reynolds. *The Keeper*. Atheneum, 1986. YA; gr. 7–10

Newton, Suzanne. *I Will Call It Georgie's Blues*. Viking, 1983. YA; gr. 7–10

Nomberg-Pryztyk, Sara. *Auschwitz: True Tales from a Grotesque Land*. Univ. of North Carolina Pr., 1985. Tr. by Roslyn Hirsch. Adult; gr. 9 up

Oneal, Zibby. *In Summer Light*. Viking Kestrel, 1985. YA; gr. 7 up

Orlev, Uri. *The Island on Bird Street*. Tr. by Hillel Halkin. Houghton, 1984. CH/YA; gr. 5–9

Orwell, George. *1984*. Harcourt, 1949. Adult; gr. 8 up

Paterson, Katherine. *The Great Gilly Hopkins*. Crowell, 1978. CH/YA; gr. 5–9

_____. *Jacob Have I Loved*. Crowell, 1980. YA; gr. 7–12.

Peck, Richard. *Are You In the House Alone?* Viking, 1976. YA; gr. 7–10

_____. *Remembering the Good Times*. Delacorte, 1985. YA; gr. 7–10

Peck, Robert Newton. *A Day No Pigs Would Die*. Knopf, 1972. Adult/YA; gr. 5 up

Pocket Poems: Selected for a Journey. Ed. by Paul B. Janeczko. Bradbury, 1985. YA/CH; gr. 5 up

Poems of Black Africa. Ed. by Wole Soyinka. Hill & Wang, 1975. Adult; gr. 8 up

Potok, Chaim. *The Chosen*. Simon & Schuster, 1967. Adult; gr. 8 up

Reflections on a Gift of Watermelon Pickle, and Other Modern Verse. Comp. by Stephen Dunning and others. Lothrop, 1966. YA/CH; gr. 6 up

Rock Voices: The Best Lyrics of an Era. Ed. with text by Matt Damsker. St. Martin's, 1980. Adult; gr. 6 up

Rossetti, Christina. "Song." *Poetical Works of Christina Rossetti*. Ed. by W. M. Rossetti. 1904. Adult; gr. 8 up

Schlee, Ann. *Ask Me No Questions*. Holt, 1976. YA/CH; gr. 6–10

Shelley, Mary. *Frankenstein*. 1818. Pennyroyal Edition. Univ. of California Pr., 1984. Adult classic; gr. 9 up

Sillitoe, Alan. *The Loneliness of the Long Distance Runner*. Knopf, 1959. Adult; gr. 9 up

Silverberg, Robert. "Caught in the Organ Draft." 1972. Title story in *Caught in the Organ Draft: Biology in Science Fiction*. Ed. by Isaac Asimov and others. Farrar, 1983. Adult; gr. 7 up

Slepian, Jan. *The Alfred Summer*. Macmillan, 1980. CH/YA; gr. 5–8

Some Haystacks Don't Even Have Any Needle, and Other Complete Modern Poems. Comp. by Stephen Dunning and others. Lothrop, 1969. YA/CH; gr. 6 up

Taylor, Mildred. *Roll of Thunder, Hear My Cry*. Dial, 1976. CH/YA; gr. 6–10

Tevis, Walter. *The Queen's Gambit*. Random, 1983. Adult; gr. 8 up

Voigt, Cynthia. *Homecoming*. Atheneum, 1981. CH/YA; gr. 6–10

_____. *The Runner*. Atheneum, 1985. YA; gr. 8–10

Wells, Rosemary. *When No One Was Looking*. Dial, 1980. YA; gr. 6–10

Why Am I Grown So Cold? Poems of the Unknowable. Comp. by Myra Cohn Livingston. Atheneum/Margaret K. McElderry, 1982. CH/YA; gr. 4 up

Willard, Nancy. *Things Invisible to See*. Knopf, 1984. Adult; gr. 8 up

Willey, Margaret. *Finding David Dolores*. Harper, 1986. CH/YA; gr. 7–10

The Yellow Canary Whose Eye Is So Black: Poems from Spanish-Speaking Latin America. Ed. and tr. by Cheli Durán. Macmillan, 1977. Adult; gr. 7 up

Zero Makes Me Hungry: A Collection of Poems for Today. Comp. by Edward Lueders and Primus St. John. Lothrop, 1976. YA; gr. 7 up

3   One Book, Many Talks

One book can provide you with a number of different booktalks. Great books aren't about one theme. You can use the same book in many ways, depending on your audience, your theme, the other books you want to integrate, and your mood. The only requirement is that you stay true to the spirit of the book.

The core of how you present the book may not change much, but you may want to vary the way you link it to other books and to your theme. If you've found a successful way to entice readers, you may be reluctant to change your talk; but sometimes variation will help prevent your feeling burned out or bored and will add excitement to your presentation.

For example, I might introduce Barbara Michaels's *Be Buried in the Rain* by talking about:

> secrets
> love that must be fought for
> an old decaying house
> a possible ghost.

A talk on Maya Angelou's autobiography *I Know Why the Caged Bird Sings* should mention the rape and her recovery, but I might focus on:

> her relationship with her beloved brother
> her adult role model
> her perception of herself as an ugly outsider
> the racism in her town.

A talk on Richard Peck's *Remembering the Good Times* must focus on friendship and suicide but might also deal with school, fathers, or divorce.

The Runner can be introduced in a character booktalk, as in chapter 2. But I might instead focus on Bullet's conflict with his father; or I might talk about running, or racism, or the outsider, or the harrowing scene where he accidentally kills his sister's dog and is shocked into realizing that he's becoming like his hated father.

The Hound of the Baskervilles may be an animal story; it is also a fine tale of terror and mystery.

The Incredible Journey is about survival, animals, and love.

This chapter shows in detail how two adult classics—*Black Boy* by Richard Wright and *Wuthering Heights* by Emily Brontë—and a contemporary book for young people—*Boy* by Roald Dahl—can each be book-talked in a number of ways.

WUTHERING HEIGHTS

There's a special pleasure in reading *Wuthering Heights* in adolescence. Several high school students have told me that it's the best book they've ever read. It's a story of violent rebellion and passion, anti-adult, anti-establishment; an agonizing depiction of self-betrayal.

I booktalk it in various ways.[1]

Sometimes I describe the opening. Making clear that the reader is supposed to be mystified, I concentrate on the drama:

On a dark and stormy night a respectable, uptight young man (even his name is Lockwood) comes to a strange, big house on the desolate moors. The dogs attack him. His host, the landowner Heathcliff, snarls at him and at Catherine, a beautiful young girl. She ignores everyone, except to snarl when spoken to. Because of a heavy snowstorm, Lockwood is trapped there, and they reluctantly give him a room for the night. Then he has a terrifying experience. He can't sleep, and he reads some old diaries he finds in his room. They were written by another Catherine, and they describe her childhood and teenage years, her passionate bond with young Heathcliff, and her misery because he is being brutally abused. As Lockwood drifts off to sleep, Cathy's ghost knocks at the window. Half-dreaming, he thinks it's the branch of a tree; and when he can't open the window, he knocks a hole through the glass and tries to seize the branch—

> instead of which, my fingers closed on the fingers of a little, ice-cold hand!

---

1. Versions of this *Wuthering Heights* discussion appeared in *Illinois Libraries* (68:385–87, June 1986) and in *Horn Book* (62:760–63, November 1986)

The intense horror of nightmare came over me; I tried to draw back my arm, but, the hand clung to it, and a most melancholy voice, sobbed,
"Let me in—let me in!"

"Who are you?" I asked struggling, meanwhile, to disengage myself.

"Catherine Linton," it replied, shiveringly, (why did I think of *Linton*? I had read *Earnshaw*, twenty times for Linton). "I'm come home, I'd lost my way on the moor!"

As it spoke, I discerned, obscurely, a child's face looking through the window—Terror made me cruel; and, finding it useless to attempt shaking the creature off, I pulled its wrist on to the broken pane, and rubbed it to and fro till the blood ran down and soaked the bed-clothes: still it wailed, "Let me in!" and maintained its tenacious grip, almost maddening me with fear.

"How can I?" I said at length. "Let *me* go, if you want me to let you in!"

The fingers relaxed, I snatched mine through the hole, hurriedly piled the books up in a pyramid against it, and stopped my ears to exclude the lamentable prayer.

I seemed to keep them closed above a quarter of an hour, yet, the instant I listened, again, there was the doleful cry moaning on!

"Begone!" I shouted, "I'll never let you in, not if you beg for twenty years!"

"It's twenty years," mourned the voice, "twenty years, I've been a waif for twenty years!" [ch. 3]

Lockwood yells for help. Heathcliff bursts in and orders Lockwood out. Then, to Lockwood's astonishment, Heathcliff tears open the window and bursts into an uncontrollable passion of tears:

"Come in! come in!" he sobbed. "Cathy, do come. Oh do—*once* more! Oh! my heart's darling, hear me *this* time—Catherine, at last!"

The next day Lockwood gets out of there as fast as he can and goes back to his own safe house, which he is renting from Heathcliff. Who are the two Catherines? What is Heathcliff's story? Why can't Cathy's ghost rest? His housekeeper, sensible Nelly Dean, was born and raised as a servant at Wuthering Heights, and she tells Lockwood the story from the beginning . . . .

Sometimes, instead of using the mysterious opening of the novel, I tell the story chronologically, as Nelly does. I describe how Catherine and Hindley's father asks them what gifts they would like from his journey to the city, and how he brings back, instead, the wild little boy Heathcliff. The father dotes on Heathcliff, and Hindley is jealous. I describe the intense bond that develops between Cathy and Heathcliff in childhood and adolescence, as they run wild in the wind and storm on the desolate moors. Then the father dies, and Hindley becomes head of the family. He abuses Heathcliff, denies him education, and banishes him to the stables.

Catherine feels all Heathcliff's pain and fury. But when a gentleman land-owner, Edgar Linton, courts her, she betrays Heathcliff—and herself—and marries Edgar.

I read from the scene where Heathcliff overhears her talking to the servant, Nelly Dean, about how it would be degrading to marry Heathcliff. Heathcliff runs away. He doesn't hear her go on to declare her love for him:

> My great miseries in this world have been Heathcliff's miseries, and I watched and felt each from the beginning; my great thought in living is himself. If all else perished, and *he* remained, I should still continue to be; and if all else remained, and he were annihilated, the Universe would turn to a mighty stranger. I should not seem a part of it. My love for Linton is like the foliage in the woods. Time will change it, I'm well aware, as winter changes the trees—my love for Heathcliff resembles the eternal rocks beneath—a source of little visible delight, but necessary. Nelly, I *am* Heathcliff—he's always, always in my mind—not as a pleasure, anymore than I am always a pleasure to myself—but, as my own being. [ch. 9]

Powerful as it is, I never start a booktalk with *Wuthering Heights,* and I do not label it a classic. I have led into—and from—*Wuthering Heights* with books about love, ghosts, rage, family conflict, mystery, self-betrayal, outsiders, a desolate setting, terror, and survival; in fact, I have used titles and themes from nearly every chapter in this book.

Janni Howker's contemporary stories for young people have the same wild, northern English setting as *Wuthering Heights.* In *The Nature of the Beast,* teenager Billy goes hunting a wild, marauding beast on the moors near his home. But part of him secretly wants to be like the beast: powerful, angry, and outside the society that has made his unemployed father and grandfather raging and bitter.

To introduce books for quite different reading interests, I sometimes use the Yorkshire setting as the link to James Herriot's autobiographical accounts of his life as a country veterinarian—humane, funny, gentle stories with vividly characterized animals and people. David Taylor's *Zoo Vet: Adventures of a Wild Animal Doctor* is also set in the north of England.

But you needn't stay that close.

A mysterious house with secrets is the link with many books, such as Virginia Hamilton's *The House of Dies Drear,* about a contemporary boy's discoveries in his Ohio house that was once an important station on the Underground Railroad.

Marilyn Singer's contemporary YA love story *The Course of True Love Never Did Run Smooth* is about teenagers Becky and Nemi, friends since childhood, who behave like Cathy in *Wuthering Heights,* betraying their deepest feelings for each other as they become infatuated with glamorous newcomers. Carson McCullers's statement about love's isolation in *The Ballad of the Sad Café* (see chapter 7) makes a startling contrast.

I may link Cathy with other ghosts who cannot rest. In Alan Garner's YA novel *The Owl Service*, two contemporary teenage boys love the same girl, and as their intense feelings mount, they find themselves acting out an age-old legend of love and revenge.

In realistic fiction and autobiography, family conflict and rage fit well with *Wuthering Heights*. There are fierce quarrels in Judith Guest's *Ordinary People*. In his autobiography, *The Big Sea*, Langston Hughes described how he faces his hatred of his father. Bette Greene's *Summer of My German Soldier* deals with child abuse in a desperately unhappy home. Then I move from family quarrels to other angry confrontations, as in the scene between high school students and armed police in William Finnegan's *Crossing the Line: A Year in the Land of Apartheid*. For a lighter note, I read the bragging insults of Nelson's aspiring-wrestler father in Bruce Stone's *Half Nelson, Full Nelson*.

An old English poem captures the tone of *Wuthering Heights*, its wild setting and all its passionate yearning:

> Western Wind, when wilt thou blow,
> The small rain down can rain?
> Christ, if my love were in my arms
> And I in my bed again!
>
> —Anon.

This is an intense note on which to end—or use it to introduce an anthology in which it appears, such as *Love Is like the Lion's Tooth*, a collection of love poems from all over the world.

BOY: TALES OF CHILDHOOD

As in the Victorian novels of childhood, Roald Dahl's autobiographical stories in *Boy* show the helpless and the innocent trying to withstand a cruel authority.[2] The stories are a mixture of fun and shivering terror, wonderful for booktalking. There's the episode when the doctor takes out the small boy's adenoids without warning and without anesthetic:

> I was too shocked and outraged to do anything but yelp. I was horrified by the huge red lumps that had fallen out of my mouth into the white basin and

---

2. Part of this discussion of *Boy* appeared in an article, "Young Adult Books: Childhood Terror," in *Horn Book* (61:598–602; September 1985).

my first thought was that the doctor had cut out the whole of the middle of my head. [p. 65]

The best story is the one about the sweetshop lady, the mean and filthy old bully Mrs. Pratchett. I read aloud her physical description and tell how the boys hate her and want to get revenge. One day they find a dead mouse, and young Dahl has a brilliant idea. They go to the sweetshop, one boy asks for a sherbet; and while Mrs. Pratchett turns away to get it, Dahl drops the mouse in the Gobstopper candy jar. He feels like a hero. The next day there is a "Closed" notice on the sweetshop door. In terror he thinks she's died of shock; he's a murderer. After school assembly, the headmaster orders the whole school to line up in the playground. Mrs. Pratchett is there. Like someone inspecting the troops, she walks up and down, until, with a yell, she picks out Dahl and his four friends. And she gets revenge: in the headmaster's study she watches with relish and spurs on the headmaster as he ferociously canes each boy in turn.

In contrast, Dahl's family life was blissful; and all the stories feel as if they have been told over and over again as family folklore.

There's the time when his nose hangs by a thread after a farcical automobile accident:

"Good heavens!" cried Dr. Dunbar. "It's been cut clean off!"

"It hurts," I moaned.

"He can't go round without a nose for the rest of his life!" the doctor said to my mother.

"It looks as though he may have to," my mother said.

"Nonsense!" the doctor told her. "I shall sew it on again."

"Can you do that?" my mother asked him.

"I can try," he answered . . . .

I woke up in my own bed with my anxious mother sitting beside me, holding my hand. "I didn't think you were ever going to come round," she said. "You've been asleep for more than eight hours."

"Did Dr. Dunbar sew my nose on again?" I asked her.

"Yes," she said.

"Will it stay on?" [pp. 97–98]

Young people relate to these stories' grim truth as well as to their often macabre comedy. Their lurking demonic terror is close to what happens in some of the best adult horror fiction.

This is one of those books that can be booktalked to all ages from about fifth grade up through adult. Depending on your audience and your theme, focus on the fun, the terror, the family love, or all three; or try two contrasting episodes. I sometimes use *Boy* as a linking book to change the tone of the booktalk. I might move from childhood terror (as in *David*

Copperfield or *The South African Quirt*) to a grim episode in *Boy*, then to a contrasting episode of Dahl family comedy, and from there to *Anastasia on Her Own* (for younger readers) or other books of cheerful domestic chaos.

BLACK BOY

So many scenes and incidents in this classic autobiography make good booktalks—dramatic, intense, immediate.

I sometimes begin with a scene that has nothing to do with Wright's being black. As a small boy, he is being bathed by his grandmother (chapter 2). He and his brother are splashing in the tub, and his grandmother is scolding and scrubbing him, when "midway between daydreaming and thinking," he lets an obscenity slip out of his mouth, "words whose meaning I did not fully know." His innocence and the adults' horror evoke wry memories in many people. We all remember that sense of bewilderment in childhood when we used language that seemed exciting without our realizing its associations for adults.

I sometimes use another childhood scene when young Wright first sees a chain gang and asks his mother to explain what seems to be a monster (chapter 2). As a straight read-aloud or partial paraphrase it has tremendous impact, with the contrast between the mother's quiet statements and the child's excited curiosity and dawning horror:

> "Why don't the white men wear stripes?"
> "They're the guards."

This episode connects well with any book about a child's bewilderment, or with the passage about the chain gang in *The Ballad of the Sad* Café.

Then I always focus on one of the book's central scenes, in which Wright as a teenager suffers brutal racism and is forced to mask his pride in himself because it antagonizes the whites. "Do you want to get killed?" asks his friend Griggs. "You act around white people as if you didn't know that they were white." I might read from the bitter scene when Griggs teaches Wright how to act subserviently on the sidewalk.

> "Then tell me how must I act?" I asked humbly. "I just want to make enough money to leave."
> "Wait and I'll tell you," he said.
> At that moment a woman and two men stepped from the jewelry store; I moved to one side to let them pass, my mind intent upon Grigg's words. Suddenly Griggs reached for my arm and jerked me violently, sending me stumbling three or four feet across the pavement. I whirled.

"What's the matter with you?" I asked.

Griggs glared at me, then laughed.

"I'm teaching you how to get out of white people's way," he said.

I looked at the people who had come out of the store; yes, they were *white,* but I had not noticed it.

"Do you see what I mean?" he asked. "White people want you out of their way." He pronounced the words slowly so that they would sink into my mind.

"I know what you mean," I breathed.

"Dick, I'm treating you like a brother," he said. "You act around white people as if you didn't know that they were white. And they *see* it."

"Oh, Christ, I can't be a slave," I said hopelessly.

"But you've got to eat," he said.

"Yes, I got to eat."

"Then start acting like it," he hammered at me, pounding his fist in his palm. "When you're in front of white people, *think* before you act, *think* before you speak. Your way of doing things is all right among *our* people, but not for *white* people. They won't stand for it."

I stared bleakly into the morning sun. I was nearing my seventeenth birthday and I was wondering if I would ever be free of this plague . . . .

"I guess you're right," I said at last. "I've got to watch myself, break myself . . . ." [ch. 9]

Another harsh scene occurs when the whites in the factory threaten young Wright and force him to leave (chapter 9). You might end by reading from his proud statement of identity when he finally manages to break free (chapter 14): "Well, the white South had never known me . . . . It had never occurred to me that I was in any way an inferior being. And no word that I had ever heard fall from the lips of southern white men had ever made me really doubt the worth of my own humanity." Or read from his own description of how books gave him "new ways of looking and seeing," showing that there was a world beyond the one in which he was trapped (chapter 13).

You can use episodes from this book with talks on outsiders, survival, war, the South, biography, friends, terror, childhood—in fact, as with all great books, it has nearly every theme you can booktalk.

BOOKS DISCUSSED

Angelou, Maya. *I Know Why the Caged Bird Sings.* Random, 1970. Adult; gr. 8 up

Brontë, Emily. *Wuthering Heights.* 1847. Adult Classic; gr. 8

Burnford, Sheila. *The Incredible Journey.* Little, Brown, 1961. Adult; gr. 5 up

Dahl, Roald. *Boy: Tales of Childhood.* Farrar, 1984. CH/YA; gr. 5 up

Dickens, Charles. *David Copperfield*. 1850. Adult classic; gr. 8 up

Doyle, Sir Arthur Conan. *The Hound of the Baskervilles. Strand Magazine*, 1901. Adult classic; gr. 8 up

Edmonds, Walter D. *The South African Quirt*. Little, Brown, 1985. Adult; gr. 8 up

Finnegan, William. *Crossing the Line: A Year in the Land of Apartheid*. Harper, 1986. Adult; gr. 9 up

Garner, Alan. *The Owl Service*. Walck, 1968. YA; gr. 7 up

Greene, Bette. *Summer of My German Soldier*. Dial, 1973. CH/YA; gr. 6–10

Guest, Judith. *Ordinary People*. Viking, 1976. Adult; gr. 8 up

Hamilton, Virginia. *The House of Dies Drear*. Macmillan, 1968. CH/YA; gr. 6–10

Herriot, James. *All Creatures Great and Small*. St. Martin's, 1972. Adult, gr. 7 up

Howker, Janni. *The Nature of the Beast*. Greenwillow, 1985. YA; gr. 7–12

Hughes, Langston. *The Big Sea: An Autobiography*. Knopf, 1940. Adult; gr. 8 up

Love Is like the Lion's Tooth: An Anthology of Love Poems. Ed. by Frances McCullough. Harper, 1984. YA; gr. 7 up

Lowry, Lois. *Anastasia on Her Own*. Houghton, 1985. CH/YA; gr. 5–8

McCullers, Carson. *The Ballad of the Sad Café and Other Stories*. Houghton, 1951. Adult Classic; gr. 10 up

Michaels, Barbara. *Be Buried in the Rain*. Atheneum, 1985. Adult; gr. 8 up

Peck, Richard. *Remembering the Good Times*. Delacorte, 1985. YA; gr. 7–10

Singer, Marilyn. *The Course of True Love Never Did Run Smooth*. Harper, 1983. YA; gr. 7–10

Stone, Bruce. *Half Nelson, Full Nelson*. Harper, 1985. YA; gr. 7–10

Taylor, David. *Zoo Vet: Adventures of a Wild Animal Doctor*. Lippincott, 1977. Adult; gr. 7 up

Voigt, Cynthia. *The Runner*. Atheneum, 1985. YA; gr. 8–10

Wright, Richard. *Black Boy*. Harper, 1945. Adult classic; gr. 7 up

4   One Theme, Many Books: War

Especially when you start booktalking, you may want to think about just one book at a time. You may want to speak for a short period and present just one or two titles that you are enthusiastic about. Many of the best booktalkers use this method with great success.

But if you want to speak longer about more books—for example, if you're going to spend a full class period with a group—you'll want to connect the books in some way.

Of course, it's fine sometimes to introduce a book with the phrase, "Another good book is . . . ," but if you do it all the time, your talk becomes choppy and unfocused.

I use a theme or themes to make the booktalk a whole and to bring together many genres, subjects, and reading levels. The unobtrusive connections help me lure readers to a wider variety of books than they would find on their own.

I like to begin with an adventure book, full of danger and excitement, to grab even the reluctant readers. World War II is always popular, with its apparently clear division between good (us) and evil (them). I often start off with a heroic battle story or with an account of ordinary young civilians caught up in the war as refugees, spies, or survivors, forced to fend for themselves without adults.

Escape from Warsaw by Ian Serraillier, based on a true story, is about a family in Nazi-occupied Warsaw during World War II. For disrespect to Hitler, the schoolmaster father, Joseph Balicki, is sent to a concentration camp. Then one day the young people, Ruth, Edek, and Bronia Balicki, watch in horror as the Nazis come to take their mother. Edek runs up to the attic where he has a gun hidden:

> The noise in the room below had stopped. Looking out of the window into

the street, he saw a Nazi van awaiting outside the front door. Two storm troopers were taking his mother down the steps, and she was struggling.

Quietly Edek lifted the window sash till it was half open. He dared not shoot in case he hit his mother. He had to wait till she was in the van and the doors were being closed.

His first shot hit a soldier in the arm. Yelling, he jumped in beside the driver. With the next two shots Edek aimed at the tyres. One punctured the rear wheel, but the van got away, skidding and roaring up the street. His other shots went wide. [p. 37]

An hour later the soldiers come back and blow up the house. Everyone assumes the young people are killed. When their father escapes from the prison camp and returns to find his home a heap of rubble, the neighbors tell him what happened. His children had not been seen since the explosion. But in fact they had worked out a daring escape, and they were surviving in the ruins of the city.

For older readers I might start with Alistair MacLean's *The Guns of Navarone*: Captain Mallory and a small group of commandos must destroy the German-held batteries in the impregnable fortress of Navarone; the lives of 1,200 British soldiers depend on their success.

Or with mature readers I might use Nicholas Monsarrat's *The Cruel Sea*: The heroism and weariness of World War II at sea are told through the experience of the men aboard a British ship that escorts the supply ships and battles the German U-boats in the stormy north Atlantic. I describe and read from one of the scenes where a ship has been torpedoed and the men are struggling in the water, choking on fuel oil, sometimes badly burned. I also talk about the personal life of First Lieutenant Lockhart: his passionate love for the beautiful young officer Julie; his strong bond with his captain, forged through shared danger.

Having caught attention with books of physical action, I introduce more subtle—but equally dramatic—fare.

Sirens and Spies by Janet Taylor Lisle shows that the division into good and evil isn't always so clear. American teenager Elsie discovers a secret that stretches back to World War II. Elsie is furious with her French violin teacher, Miss Fitch. Until now there had always been a special tie between them, and talented Elsie had always wanted to be like Miss Fitch. But now Elsie has stopped her lessons and won't have anything to do with her teacher. The reason is a photograph Elsie found one day in the library. She had been reading a book about World War II, with horrifying pictures of injury and destruction. Then she saw a photograph of a parade in a French town after the defeat of the Nazis. Women accused of being collaborators with German lovers had had their heads shaved and were being driven in a cart through jeering crowds—and one of the women was Miss Fitch. Elsie is finally persuaded by her sister to ask Miss Fitch what happened.

The truth about the war in Vietnam is what worries contemporary Kentucky teenager Samantha ("Sam") in *In Country* by Bobbie Ann Mason. Sam's father died in Vietnam before she was born. After her high school graduation she becomes obsessed with finding out about that war and about her father. She hates to think about the brutal things her father did in Vietnam. Then one day, after she's been sitting in the shopping mall reading his war diary, she wonders how *she* might behave under fire:

> What would make people want to kill? If the U.S.A. sent her to a foreign country, with a rifle and a heavy backpack, could she root around in the jungle, sleep in the mud, and shoot at strangers? How did the Army get boys to do that? Why was there war? [p. 208]

You can talk about how Sam watches M*A*S*H reruns on television with her boyfriend and her Vietnam-vet uncle; then you can lead from M*A*S*H to two contemporary classics of savage, absurdist antiwar humor: *Catch-22* by Joseph Heller and *Slaughterhouse Five* by Kurt Vonnegut. If you think your audience has had enough literal warfare, Sam's search for her father can lead into some of the books on father-daughter confrontations and family wars, such as Cyra McFadden's autobiographical *Rain or Shine*, about her pain and anger at being rejected by her father.

Or, from Sam's hatred of the war, I might move to Remarque's antiwar classic *All Quiet on the Western Front,* the bitter German novel about young men in World War I, sent by false patriotism to fight for a cause they know nothing about, against an enemy just like them. In spare, laconic style, accessible to most junior high and high school readers, a young soldier tells the story of himself and his school classmates in the trenches. There are dozens of episodes for booktalking: terse, heartbreaking scenes that communicate the boys' loss of innocence as they face suffering and horror. The novel needs the briefest of historical introductions about trench warfare, with soldiers on both sides unaware of why they were fighting.

To communicate the false patriotism that sent them to battle, I tell about their schoolmaster who exhorted them to "join up" and fight. Then I read the episode about Joseph Behm, who died in agony in No Man's Land:

> There was, indeed, one of us who hesitated and did not want to fall into line. That was Joseph Behm, a plump, homely fellow. But he did allow himself to be persuaded, otherwise he would have been ostracized. And perhaps more of us thought as he did, but no one could very well stand out, because at the time even one's parents were ready with the word "coward"; no one had the vaguest idea what we were in for . . . .

Strange to say, Behm was one of the first to fall. He got hit in the eye during an attack, and we left him lying for dead. We couldn't bring him with us, because we had to come back helter-skelter. In the afternoon suddenly we heard him call, and saw him crawling about in No Man's Land. He had only been knocked unconscious. Because he could not see, and was mad with pain, he failed to keep under cover, and so was shot down before anyone could go and fetch him in. [ch. 1, sec. 3]

The narrator attacks those who sent young boys to their deaths with talk of glory:

While they continued to write and talk, we saw the wounded and dying. While they taught that duty to one's country is the greatest thing, we already knew that death-throes are stronger. But for all that we were no mutineers, no deserters, no cowards—they were very free with all these expressions. We loved our country as much as they; we went courageously into every action; but also we distinguished the false from true, we had suddenly learned to see. And we saw that there was nothing of their world left. We were all at once terribly alone; and alone we must see it through. [ch. 1, sec. 3]

Or I read from the scene (ch. 1, sec. 4) where the boys visit their wounded schoolmate Kemmerich, and realize he is dying. His leg has been amputated. One of the boys, Muller, covets the dying boy's boots—not because Muller does not feel grief for his friend, but because Kemmerich will not use his legs again and good boots are scarce.

There is the scene (ch. 2, sec. 5) when the narrator, Paul Baümer, is with Kemmerich as he dies in the chaos of the dressing station; or I read the scene in which Paul, back on leave, visits Kemmerich's mother. Sometimes I use one of the scenes of battle or attack by poison gas.

Wilfred Owen, a young British poet who was killed near the end of World War I, wrote this about exhausted soldiers trudging back to base when they are hit by a poison-gas attack:

Bent double, like old beggars under sacks,
Knock-kneed, coughing like hags, we cursed through sludge,
Till on the haunting flares we turned our backs
And towards our distant rest began to trudge.
Men marched asleep. Many had lost their boots
But limped on, blood-shod. All went lame; all blind;
Drunk with fatigue; deaf even to the hoots
Of gas shells dropping softly behind.

Gas! GAS! Quick, boys!—An ecstasy of fumbling,
Fitting the clumsy helmets just in time;
But someone still was yelling out and stumbling,
And flound'ring like a man in fire or lime . . .
Dim, through the misty panes and thick green light,

> As under a green sea, I saw him drowning.
> In all my dreams, before my helpless sight,
> He plunges at me, guttering, choking, drowning.

This is from the poem "Dulce et Decorum Est." Because the Latin will close off the poem to most readers, I usually read only the first stanzas and give the title afterwards. I just lead straight into the poem from Remarque. The episode with Kemmerich's boots links well with the first stanza; the gas attack links with the second.

Milton Meltzer's *Ain't Gonna Study War No More*, a history of pacifism in the United States, shows that the pacifists had a lot of support for their stand against World War I. I sometimes tell one of the heroic stories of passive resistance. But Meltzer also depicts the pacifists' dilemma when faced with a righteous cause. Would you have fought in the American Revolution? Was passive resistance any good against slavery in the Civil War? (To lighten the tone, you might like to quote Mark Twain's quip from "A Private History of a Campaign That Failed" about his unheroic role in the Civil War: "incapacitated by fatigue through persistent retreating.") Would you not use violence against the Nazi Holocaust? Against apartheid?

Each of these questions can lead into a different book.

In *Freedom Rising*, young Harvard graduate James North describes how he spent four years in South Africa, traveling all over and speaking with people of all colors and backgrounds. He interviews racists, victims and fighters, and combines the personal stories with political and historical background. A young man talks about his resistance under torture:

> "I still wasn't going to tell them anything. I can't explain . . . you have to be in that position yourself. I had *nothing* to lose. All I wanted was my dignity as a human being. I would keep that. I told them so. 'If I die, I die,' I said. Also, I knew I had my own foolishness to blame for getting caught. I felt I had to endure." [p. 58]

This young man, Mandla Mazibuko, came from a very religious home, and had always believed in nonviolence. But he changed; he wanted to leave and join the guerilla army.

> "I would not like to kill," he told me in mid-1979. "But I am not afraid to die. I read a book once by a revolutionary from East Africa, which said we must not be afraid of religion. We must be prepared to be like Jesus and die for the people. We must resist evil to avoid becoming part of it." [p. 59]

In *Night*, one of the starkest of all autobiographical accounts, Elie Wiesel describes the nightmare terror when as a young boy in Hungary during World War II he was taken with his father and other Jews to

Buchenwald concentration camp, and how he watched his father break down and die there.

Myron Levoy's *Alan and Naomi* is about a young Jewish boy in New York during World War II who struggles to find meaning in the overwhelming evil of the Holocaust. Alan's parents ask him to help Naomi, who lives in the upstairs apartment. She has been mentally disturbed since she watched her father beaten to death by Nazis in France. Alan doesn't want to go near her:

> "I won't do it. I have enough problems the way it is. Some of the guys call me sissy sometimes! . . . I got one friend on the block, that's all. And he'll quit on me! She's a girl! And she's crazy! . . .
> "Dad, I can't! It's not fair! Don't make me do this. *Please!*" [p. 20]

But his father makes an appeal:

> "No, we can't force you. But—allow me one but. In our life, Alan, sometimes when we're young, sometimes when we're old, in our life, once or twice, we're called upon to do something we can't do . . . . Why do we do it? It's a mystery. Maybe to prove that what we *are* is something a little more than what we think we are."

Reluctantly Alan agrees, and he visits Naomi daily, talking to her through his old puppet. After days and days of compulsively tearing paper, she finally begins to answer him through her doll. Although Alan and Naomi are only twelve, junior high and high school readers are moved by the horror of Naomi's experience, by Alan's moral struggle, and by the integrity of the bleak ending.

The threat of nuclear holocaust hangs over us today. Here you can include fiction, personal accounts, science, history.

In *Day One,* Peter Wyden looks at the history of how the bomb was developed—the gathering of the great scientists at Los Alamos, the race to be first, the scientists' personal stories, the technology and the politics—and the aftermath. He describes a recent interview with the physicist Seth Neddermeyer. His achievement of plutonium implosion at Los Alamos had been pivotal. Now he was in torment:

> "I get overwhelmed by a feeling of terrible guilt when I think about the history of the bomb," Neddermeyer said. Near tears, he wondered aloud: "This is what bugs me more than anything else—I don't remember having any strong feelings about [the bombings] at the time. I guess I just got caught up in the mindless hysteria." [Warner ed., p. 366]

Wyden describes what happened in the plane, the *Enola Gay,* from which the first bomb was dropped. There was elation; but the copilot wrote in his record: "My God, what have we done?" (Warner ed., p. 247).

In horrifying detail, Wyden tells of what happened in Hiroshima, immediately, and long afterwards. And he looks at the terror of the present arms race.

Space war against aliens is the threat in Orson Scott Card's *Ender's Game*. Ender, child genius, is removed from his family to begin his training in a harsh military school. His teachers hope to make him the supreme commander to lead the earth's armies in space against the alien forces. He is trained on exciting computer-simulated war games and in fierce confrontations with other students. Though he is a loving person, he learns violence, even to kill when necessary.

Contemporary young people must join the age-old battle against the forces of the Dark in *The Dark Is Rising,* Susan Cooper's five-part fantasy series. Will Stanton is the "seventh son of a seventh son," and as his family noisily celebrates Christmas, his hidden powers are revealed to him: he is one of a special circle who must undertake a quest in the fight against the Dark powers that threaten once again to take over the world.

Sometimes a book about the conflict in a family (or between lovers, or inside one person) can be as intense as an account of world warfare. With any version of that link you can change back smoothly to realistic fiction and integrate books about family or lovers' quarrels—savage or funny—or about individual struggle.

In James Baldwin's *Go Tell It on the Mountain,* John's fight with his father is about the black man's view of himself, but it is also about a teenager's struggle against his parent's self-righteous, brutal authority. The conflict is presented with complexity and passion.

I use the scene where John comes home to find that his older brother, Roy, has been stabbed in a gang fight with whites. For a naked moment John sees that his father wishes it were he, John, who had been hurt and not the favored elder son. As John comes home he meets his sister, who is relishing the excitement:

> "What happened?" he whispered.
>
> She stared at him in astonishment, and a certain wild joy. He thought again that he really did not like his sister. Catching her breath, she blurted out, triumphantly: "Roy got stabbed with a knife!" and rushed into the living-room.
>
> Roy got stabbed with a knife. Whatever this meant, it was sure that his father would be at his worst tonight. John walked slowly into the living-room.
>
> His father and mother, a small basin of water between them, knelt by the sofa where Roy lay, and his father was washing the blood from Roy's forehead.

... Then his father turned and looked at him.

"Where you been, boy," he shouted, "all this time? Don't you know you's needed here at home?"

More than his words, his face caused John to stiffen instantly with malice and fear. His father's face was terrible in anger, but now there was more than anger in it. John saw now what he had never seen there before, except in his own vindictive fantasies: a kind of wild, weeping terror that made the face seem younger, and yet at the same time unutterably older and more cruel. And John knew, in the moment his father's eyes swept over him, that he hated John because John was not lying on the sofa where Roy lay. John could scarcely meet his father's eyes, and yet, briefly, he did, saying nothing, feeling in his heart an odd sensation of triumph, and hoping in his heart that Roy, to bring his father low, would die. [Dell/Laurel ed., p. 41]

Mexican-American Chato in Danny Santiago's *Famous All over Town* is pressured by his father and by the neighborhood gang to be macho and violent. He remembers a brutal scene when he must help beat up a rival gang member:

that time four of us stomped Blackie. There he was on the pavement while we worked him over with our boots. He might be Sierra and no denying he once busted a baseball bat on Kiko from behind, but all bloody on the pavement and screaming and begging for his life like a baby, it made me sick. I had to kneel beside the telephone pole and vomit in the gutter. What was wrong with me that win or lose I couldn't feel good about it either way? [p. 61]

But sad as it is, this book has a tender, funny tone. On his fourteenth birthday Chato must slaughter a chicken to prove he's a man, using his father's special knife:

It took place on a hot Saturday in September.

"Here's your present."

My father slapped his chicken-killer knife into my hand. It was ground down thin as a needle and had a razor edge. Nobody but him was allowed to touch it.

"Huh?" I asked.

"Fourteen years makes a man, so prove yourself."

"Me?" I asked.

"Why not?" he said. "You seen me do it often enough."

"When?" I asked.

"When I tell you to," he told me crossly, "and quit looking so green in the face."

My father was quite famous for his chicken killing. [p. 8]

The war between brothers can be both violent and loving. In S. E. Hinton's *Tex,* fifteen-year-old Tex and his older brother Mace have always gotten along pretty well in their ramshackle house in Oklahoma. Their mother is dead, their father has been gone a long time. Tex keeps waiting for his father to come back; he's sure it won't be long. But one day Tex comes home from school to find that Mace has sold his own horse and Tex's beloved horse, Negrito—to pay for groceries and heat. In his anguish, Tex hits out at his brother, who beats him up. After the fight,

> "Lookit, Tex, it wasn't you—I mean, I didn't aim to take it out on you like that."
> I didn't know what he was talking about and I didn't care.
> "I'm going to get my horse back," I said. "Pop wouldn't let you sell those horses if he were here."
> "Pop isn't here!" Mason shouted. "Can't you get it through your thick skull that all this happened because Pop isn't here!"
> I flinched a little. For a second I thought I felt his hand on the back of my hair, then he muttered, "Well, hell."
> Pretty soon I heard the back door slam and the pickup engine start. He'd go drive up and down the highway for a while. He always did that when he was mad.
> I couldn't seem to stop crying. I cried because I was hurting and because I wanted to kill Mace, and he was my only brother and I didn't really want to kill him. I cried because Mason had never beaten me up before. Mostly we got along pretty good. Finally I thought about Negrito being gone and Pop being gone and I bawled like a baby. I never cried much before and I wasn't used to it and I didn't know how to stop. [p. 14]

In Lois Lowry's *A Summer to Die,* Meg and her older sister Molly used to have their own rooms. "It didn't really make us better friends, but it gave us a chance to ignore each other more." They're very different, and it's hard now that they have to share a room, living in an old house in the country for a year. One day Meg watches in astonishment as her sister takes a piece of white chalk and angrily draws a line on the rug:

> she kept right on drawing the line up the wall across the wallpaper with its blue flowers. She stood on her desk and drew the line up to the ceiling, and then she went back to the other side of the room and stood on her bed and drew the line right up to the ceiling on that wall, too. Very neatly. Good thing it was Molly who drew it; if I had tried, it would have been a mess, a wavy line and off center. But Molly is very neat.
> Then she put the chalk back in the dish, sat down on her bed, and picked up her book. But before she started to read again, she looked over at me (I was still standing there amazed, not believing that she had drawn the line at all) and said, "There. Now be as much of a slob as you want, only keep your mess on your side. *This* side is *mine.*" [Bantam ed., p. 2]

Meg envies Molly's self-confidence, beauty, and popularity. Then Molly becomes very ill and everything changes.

For a change of tone I sometimes use the funny, upbeat gang story, *Fast Sam, Cool Clyde, and Stuff,* by Walter Dean Myers. Especially for junior high, the insults scene never fails.

Binky, "the baddest dude on the block," likes the same girl as Robin, a tough guy from another street. Robin insults Binky, who at first seems to take it:

> it seemed Binky was backing out of a fight. But just then Binky made his comeback.
>
> "Look, Robin, I don't want to argue with you. I believe in equal opportunity for people who've been in terrible accidents, and from the way you look, I can see your face has been in just about the most terrible accident I've ever seen."
>
> Everybody jumped up behind that. Binky was going to stand up to Robin after all.
>
> "What did you say, man?" Robin's boys backed off because they knew the fight was on.
>
> "I said if you were any uglier they'd put your face in a museum and sell tickets to gorillas." Binky stood up. "The worse thing I could say about your mama is that you're her son. And hasn't anybody told you yet that that toe-jam you keep between your teeth don't do nothin' for your breath?" [Avon/ Flare ed., p. 18]

This contrasts well with a brutal gang story such as *The Chocolate War.*

For contrast after all the books on war and conflict, I might end with Ed Ochester's beautiful poem of reconciliation, "The Gift," about a stray cat that brings a quarreling family together.

> One day
> as I was lying on the lawn
> dreaming of the Beautiful
> and my wife was justifiably bitching
>   out the window
> at my shiftlessness and
> the baby was screaming
> because I wouldn't let him
> eat my cigarettes,
> a tiger cat leaped over the fence,
> smiled at my wife,
> let the baby pull his tail,
> hummed like a furry dynamo
> as I stroked him.
>
> My wife took the car to get him some food,
> my son began to sing his wordless song,
> and I wrote a poem in the sand.

Now God give every man who's hopeless
a beautiful wife,
an infant son who sings,
and the gift of a sweet-faced cat.

The poem is in Paul Janeczko's YA anthology *Poetspeak*, in which several contemporary poets choose and comment on their work. After reading the poem, I read briefly from Ochester's comments:

> What struck me as important, and the reason I wanted to get it into a poem, is that so much of our lives is like this. What turns out to be important is what you hadn't expected and couldn't have planned on, and that very often in itself seems inconsequential . . . . The three people in "The Gift" are momentarily silly because they're so much locked into their private patterns that they forget for the moment that they love one another. The animal is the catalyst—who would have predicted it?—that gets them past a bad time. [pp. 158–59]

MORE WAR

Additional suggestions for a variety of books that can fit well with the theme of war:

Avi. *The Fighting Ground.* Lippincott, 1984. CH/YA; gr. 5–8
   A deceptively simple story about thirteen-year-old Jonathan, who can't wait to join the fighting during the Revolutionary War, but who discovers slaughter and muddle, and conflict in himself, where he thought there'd be glory.

Cooney, Caroline. *Don't Blame the Music.* Putnam/Pacer, 1986. YA; gr. 8–12
   Susan's suburban, preppy life is blown apart when her older sister, a failed rock star, returns home, defeated, vicious, violent, and in terrible pain.
   See Stephanie Zvirin's discussion of this and other "sister wars" in her YA Connection article, "Sisters, Sisters, Sisters," *Booklist* 83:216 (October 1, 1986).

Frank, Rudolf. *No Hero for the Kaiser.* Tr. from the German by Patricia Crampton. Lothrop, 1986. CH/YA; gr. 6–10
   First published in Germany in 1931, publicly burned by Hitler, and only translated into English in 1986, this novel about fourteen-year-old Jan caught in the cross fire of World War I has the stark, concrete style and urgent antiwar message of *All Quiet on the Western Front.*

Read from the chapters that begin with the fascinating technical detail about artillery and tactics and then explode into slaughter, as in the chapter about shrapnel that ends with Jan's discovery of a trench of corpses (p. 75).

Hemingway, Ernest. *A Farewell to Arms*. Scribner's, 1929. Adult; gr. 9 up
In the muddle and horror on the Italian front during World War I, an American ambulance driver is wounded and falls passionately in love with a Scottish nurse.
(This fits just as well with the theme of love.)

Macaulay, David. *Castle*. Houghton, 1977. CH/YA; gr. 5 up
Detailed and beautiful drawings and a clear, informative, sometimes humorous text show the construction of a typical thirteenth-century Welsh castle; the book ends with an exciting siege.

Mahy, Margaret. *The Changeover: A Supernatural Romance*. Atheneum/ Margaret K. McElderry, 1984. YA/CH; gr. 6–10
With the help of an older boy who loves her, Laura "changes over" into a witch to fight the evil forces that are attacking her little brother.

Newton, Suzanne. *I Will Call It Georgie's Blues*. Viking, 1983. YA; gr. 7–10
The town minister bullies his family. Fifteen-year-old Neal has a secret escape in his music from the rage and pain of his home. But his fragile little brother is breaking down.

Olson, Ray. "Nonviolence: The Tradition of Gandhi and King." *Booklist* 83:108 (September 15, 1986).
An annotated bibliography that includes sermons, journalism, manuals, biographies, and topical anthologies. Prepared by Books for Adults Assistant Editor Ray Olson.

Westall, Robert. *The Machine Gunners*. Greenwillow, 1976. CH/YA; gr. 6–10
After an air raid during World War II, a group of young people in the north of England take a machine gun from a crashed German plane. Led by Chas McGill, they build a secret place for the gun and prepare to use it.

BOOKS DISCUSSED

Baldwin, James. *Go Tell It on the Mountain*. Knopf, 1953. Dell/Laurel, 1985. Adult; gr. 9 up

Card, Orson Scott. *Ender's Game*. Tor, 1985. Adult; gr. 8 up

Cooper, Susan. *The Dark Is Rising*. Atheneum/Margaret K. McElderry, 1973. CH/
YA; gr. 5 up

Cormier, Robert. *The Chocolate War*. Pantheon, 1974. YA; gr. 7 up

Heller, Joseph. *Catch-22*. Simon & Schuster, 1961. Adult; gr. 10 up

Hinton, S. E. *Tex*. Delacorte, 1979. YA; gr. 6–10

Levoy, Myron. *Alan and Naomi*. Harper, 1977. CH/YA; gr. 6–10

Lisle, Janet Taylor. *Sirens and Spies*. Bradbury, 1985. CH/YA; gr. 7–10

Lowry, Lois. *A Summer to Die*. Houghton, 1977. CH/YA; gr. 6–10

McFadden, Cyra. *Rain or Shine*. Knopf, 1986. Adult; gr. 8 up

MacLean, Alistair. *The Guns of Navarone*. Doubleday, 1957. Adult; gr. 8 up

Mason, Bobbie Ann. *In Country*. Harper, 1985. Adult; gr. 8 up

Meltzer, Milton. *Ain't Gonna Study War No More*. Harper, 1985. YA; gr. 7–10

Monsarrat, Nicholas. *The Cruel Sea*. Knopf, 1951. Adult; gr. 11 up

Myers, Walter Dean. *Fast Sam, Cool Clyde, and Stuff*. Viking, 1975; Avon/Flare,
1979. CH/YA; gr. 6 up

North, James. *Freedom Rising*. Macmillan, 1985. Adult; gr. 8 up

Owen, Wilfred. "Dulce et Decorum Est." 1917. *The Complete Poems and Fragments*.
Ed. by Jon Stallworthy. London: Chatto & Windus, 1983. Adult; gr. 8
up

Poetspeak: In Their Work, about Their Work. Ed. by Paul B. Janeczko. Bradbury, 1983.
YA; gr. 7–12

Remarque, Erich Maria. *All Quiet on the Western Front*. Little, Brown, 1929. Tr. from
German by A. W. Wheen. Adult classic; gr. 8 up

Santiago, Danny. *Famous All Over Town*. Simon & Schuster, 1983. Adult; gr. 9
up

Serraillier, Ian. *Escape from Warsaw*. Scholastic, 1956. (Published in England as *The
Silver Sword*.) CH/YA; gr. 5–8

Twain, Mark. *A Pen Warmed Up in Hell: Mark Twain in Protest*. Harper, 1972.
Adult; gr. 8 up

Vonnegut, Kurt. *Slaughterhouse Five, or the Children's Crusade*. Delacorte, 1969.
Adult; gr. 10 up

Wiesel, Elie. *Night*. Tr. from French by Stella Rodway. Hill & Wang, 1960. Adult;
gr. 8 up

Wyden, Peter. *Day One: Before Hiroshima and After*. Simon & Schuster, 1984. Adult;
gr. 8 up

Part 2

Booktalks and More

In chapters 5 through 9, some booktalks are arranged by theme. Each theme-chapter includes talks and suggestions for talks on classics—traditional and contemporary, adult and YA—as well as on other high-quality books.

Sometimes, as in the chapter on terror, the books are linked. But in general, within each chapter and among the chapters, the organization is tentative, always shifting.

The annotations in the "More . . ." sections include some additional titles for you to consider booktalking with each theme. These lists also demonstrate the wide range of possible approaches within each theme; and they bring in good popular titles, adult and YA, that work well with the classic stories.

Friends have pushed me to include their favorite books. They often remember where they first found a special book and when, or who gave it to them, and which parts are special, and how it exploded in their lives. How could you leave out *Huck Finn,* they say, or Steinbeck, Salinger, Betsy Byars, Sue Ellen Bridgers, Arthur C. Clarke; *The Outsiders, A Wrinkle in Time, Sons and Lovers, The Glass Menagerie, To Kill a Mockingbird, A Wizard of Earthsea*?

The answer is that it was hard leaving out those books and dozens of others. There isn't room here for more than a fraction of the great books to share with young people.

Both the longer talks and the annotations are only examples and approaches to start you off in developing your own talks in your own way with your own combinations.

Booktalk your own touchstone books, those that are part of you. Share your pleasure.

5 Animals

London, Jack. *White Fang*
Doyle, Sir Arthur Conan. *Hound of the Baskervilles*
McCaffrey, Anne. *Dragonsong*
Keyes, Daniel. *Flowers for Algernon*
Orwell, George. *Animal Farm*
Fox, Paula. *One-Eyed Cat*
Eckert, Allan. *Incident at Hawk's Hill*
Herriot, James. *All Creatures Great and Small*
Bond, Nancy. *A Place to Come Back To*
Lawrence, D. H. "Snake"

The subject of animals grabs the interest of most young people. It allows you to include a wide range of books in a variety of genres for all kinds of readers. It unifies wilderness adventure, family stories, science fiction, mystery, fantasy, poetry, ethology, and I even dare to include a book about someone who doesn't love animals. Because of the high-interest topic, much adult material and much nonfiction on this subject is accessible to young people.

This is one subject where I sometimes include more than one traditional classic in the same booktalk. *Hound of the Baskervilles, Animal Farm,* and *White Fang* are so different from each other and so interesting to young people that at least two could be introduced in the same talk.

Several books discussed in other chapters could be integrated here, such as Orlev's *Island on Bird Street* (a Holocaust-survival story, where the Jewish boy's sole companion in his hideout is a white mouse) and S. E. Hinton's *Tex* (where Tex's elder brother sells their beloved horses to pay for groceries).

And it works the other way too. Animal stories can be integrated into other theme booktalks—on survival, family, outsiders, love, biography, etc.

London, Jack. *White Fang*. 1906. Adult classic; gr. 7 up

In the Alaskan wilderness, a savage frozen desolation, a string of wolfish dogs is pulling a sled. One man toils in front, another behind the sled. On the sled is a coffin with the body of an English lord the two men have been sent to collect for burial. It is 50 degrees below. The vast silence is all around them as the few hours of daylight end. Suddenly the silence is broken by the hunting cries of a pack of hungry wolves. The wolves come closer, trailing them. At night the darkness presses in around their camp from every side, and they see a circle of wolves' gleaming eyes, burning in the darkness just beyond the firelight. They're almost out of ammunition—only three cartridges left. They discover that a she-wolf, half dog, is coming into their camp each night acting as decoy, luring away one of the dogs to be food for the wolves—until only three dogs are left of the original six. When the fourth dog leaves in broad daylight, Bill, one of the men, loses control, takes the gun, and goes after the she-wolf in a fury. Henry, the man back at camp, hears a shot, then two shots in rapid succession, and he knows the ammunition is gone. Then he hears a great outcry of snarls and yelps, then nothing. "Silence settled down again over the lonely land" (ch. 3). There was no need for him to go and see what happened. Then there is one man with two dogs and the coffin alone against the wolves. They form a circle around him, waiting, distanced only by the fire he keeps blazing.

> With night came horror. Not only were the starving wolves growing bolder, but lack of sleep was telling upon Henry. He dozed despite himself, crouching by the fire, the blankets about his shoulders, the axe between his knees, and on either side a dog pressing close against him. He awoke once and saw in front of him, not a dozen feet away, a big gray wolf, one of the largest of the pack. And even as he looked, the brute deliberately stretched himself after the manner of a lazy dog, yawning full in his face and looking upon him with a possessive eye, as if, in truth, he were merely a delayed meal that was soon to be eaten.
>
> This certitude was shown by the whole pack. Fully a score he could count, staring hungrily at him or calmly sleeping in the snow. They reminded him of children gathered about a spread table and waiting permission to begin to eat. And he was the food they were to eat! He wondered how and when the meal would begin.
>
> As he piled wood on the fire he discovered an appreciation of his own body which he had never felt before. He watched his moving muscles and was interested in the cunning mechanism of his fingers. By the light of the fire he crooked his fingers slowly and repeatedly, now one at a time, now all

together, spreading them wide or making quick gripping movements. He studied the nail formation, and prodded the fingertips, now sharply, and again softly, gauging the while the nerve sensations produced. It fascinated him, and he grew suddenly fond of this subtle flesh of his that worked so beautifully and smoothly and delicately. Then he would cast a glance of fear at the wolf-circle drawn expectantly about him, and like a blow the realization would strike him that this wonderful body of his, this living flesh, was no more than so much meat, a quest of ravenous animals, to be torn and slashed by their hungry fangs. [ch. 3]

This may be too long a passage to read aloud for most groups. You may want to choose a few of the most highly charged sentences.

Doyle, Sir Arthur Conan. *The Hound of the Baskervilles*. 1901. Adult classic; gr. 8 up

A terrifying legendary monster that roams the bleak stormy moors is the basis of the Sherlock Holmes mystery *The Hound of the Baskervilles*. The story begins in Holmes's cozy rooms in Baker Street, London, where the famous detective and his assistant, Dr. Watson, receive a visitor with a strange story. He is a country doctor, Dr. Mortimer, and he wants Sherlock Holmes to investigate the recent death of Lord Baskerville near his home on Dartmoor. The newspapers say that Lord Baskerville died of a heart attack. But that isn't the whole story, says Mortimer, and he tells of the ancient curse of the Baskervilles:

Long ago, a wicked Lord Hugo Baskerville kidnapped a beautiful young girl and locked her in a room in his mansion while he and his companions feasted and drank. She escaped and ran out onto the moor. When Sir Hugo discovered this, in his fury he loosed his hunting hounds to chase her, then raced after her on his black mare. By the time his companions found him on the moor,

> The moon was shining bright upon the clearing, and there in the center lay the unhappy maid where she had fallen, dead of fear and of fatigue. But it was not the sight of her body, not yet was it that of the body of Hugo Baskerville lying near her which raised the hair upon the heads of these three daredevil roysterers, but it was that, standing over Hugo, and plucking at his throat, there stood a foul thing, a great, black beast, shaped like a hound, yet larger than any hound that ever mortal eye has rested upon. And even as they looked the thing tore the throat out of Hugo Baskerville, on which, as it turned its blazing eyes and dripping jaws upon them, the three shrieked with fear and rode for dear life, still screaming across the moor . . . . [ch. 2]

Ever since then, the doctor tells Sherlock Holmes, the lords of the Baskerville family seem to have been cursed, their deaths sudden, bloody, and mysterious.

Sherlock Holmes looks bored: "That's a fairytale," he says, "What's it got to do with the death of the latest Lord Baskerville? He died of a heart attack in the grounds of his home."

Dr. Mortimer answers in a whisper: When he examined the body on the night of the death, he found nearby—the footprints of a gigantic hound.

Note: The read-aloud is vivid and dramatic. It also shows that the language isn't easy.

McCaffrey, Anne. *Dragonsong*. Atheneum, 1976. YA; gr. 6 up

In Anne McCaffrey's fantasy series, *The Dragonriders of Pern,* the people on the planet Pern have developed huge dragons to help them survive. The dragons breathe out tongues of fire to destroy the menace that threatens the planet. The dragons and their riders are telepathically joined for life.

In *Dragonsong* the young girl, Menolly, desperately wants to play music and compose. But her father forbids it: mere girls can't hold the important position of musician-harper in their society. Frustrated and lonely, she runs away. She takes refuge in a cave, where she sees a group of nine beautiful little fire-lizards—small relatives of the dragons—hatch out of their eggs. She feeds them and comforts them: this "impresses" them, which means that they become telepathically joined to her—they can understand what she is thinking. They love her music and she teaches them to sing. Then, in a dangerous time, she is rescued by a dragon and his rider and taken with the fire-lizards to the place of the great dragonriders.

Keyes, Daniel. *Flowers for Algernon*. Harcourt, 1966. Adult; gr. 8 up

Charlie has a special bond with a white mouse called Algernon. Algernon is part of a scientific experiment that has made him super-intelligent through brain surgery. Charlie is a mentally disabled young man, and in his own words he tells how he has agreed to have that surgery done to *his* brain, in the first such experiment on a human. He knows that the surgery could fail, or it could succeed for a while, and then leave him worse off; but he wants to risk it—one of the reasons why he is such a good subject for the experiment is that he's so motivated; "After the operashun Im gonna try to be smart. Im gonna try awful hard."

> Prof Nemur says if it werks good and its perminent they will make other pepul like me smart also. Maybe pepul all over the werld. And he said that meens I'm doing something grate for sience and Ill be famus and my name will go down in the books. I dont care so much about beeing famus. I just want to be smart like other pepul so I can have lots of frends who like me.
> [Bantam, p. 9]

After the surgery Charlie describes how the doctors test him and test him. At first in Charlie's contests with Algernon, the mouse always wins. Then gradually Charlie beats Algernon, and we see from Charlie's writing that he become superbrilliant, more than his doctors, and he falls in love. But then he watches in anguish as Algernon begins to behave strangely . . . . (In order not to mislead students about this book, I might be telling too much of the story. You might choose to leave out the change in Algernon.)

Orwell, George. *Animal Farm*. Harcourt, 1946. Adult classic; gr. 6 up]

The animals on the farm rebel. Why should they work so hard and allow the humans to reap all the benefit? They chase the people off the farm and, led by the pigs, they set up a new society. Their Seven Commandments are:

1. Whatever goes upon two legs is an enemy.
2. Whatever goes upon four legs, or has wings, is a friend.
3. No animal shall wear clothes.
4. No animal shall sleep in a bed.
5. No animal shall drink alcohol.
6. No animal shall kill any other animal.
7. All animals are equal.[Signet ed., p. 33]

The animals work very hard and are happier than they dreamed possible. With the example of the great working-horse, Boxer, they all work as never before. But gradually things change; the pigs gain power over the others, and the commandments are altered. Now the last one reads: "All animals are equal. But some animals are more equal than others" (p. 123).

The book is a funny fable, but it is also a grim picture of a totalitarian society, and along the way you get to care deeply about the individual animals. There's a moving scene when Boxer, the beloved, hardworking horse becomes weak and ill:

> It was in the middle of the day when the van came to take him away. The animals were all at work weeding turnips under the supervision of a pig, when they were astonished to see Benjamin come galloping from the direction of the farm buildings, braying at the top of his voice. It was the first time that they had ever seen Benjamin excited—indeed, it was the first time that anyone had ever seen him gallop. "Quick, quick!" he shouted. "Come at once! They're taking Boxer away!" Without waiting for orders from the pig, the animals broke off work and raced back to the farm buildings. Sure enough, there in the yard was a large closed van, drawn by two horses, with lettering on its side and a sly-looking man in a low-crowned bowler hat sitting on the driver's seat. And Boxer's stall was empty.

The animals crowded around the van. "Good-bye, Boxer!" they chorused, "good-bye!"

"Fools! Fools!" shouted Benjamin, prancing round them and stamping the earth with his small hoofs. "Fools! Do you not see what is written on the side of that van?"

That gave the animals pause, and there was a hush. Muriel began to spell out the words. But Benjamin pushed her aside and in the midst of a deadly silence he read:

"'Alfred Simmonds, Horse Slaughterer and Glue Boiler, Willingdon. Dealer in Hides and Bonemeal. Kennels Supplied.' Do you not understand what that means? They are taking Boxer to the knacker's!"

A cry of horror burst from all the animals. [pp. 112–13]

Fox, Paula. *One-Eyed Cat*. Bradbury, 1984. CH/YA; gr. 5 up

Ned Wallis is the minister's only son. He knows he is loved by his gentle father and his witty, irreverent mother. His mother is ill, crippled with rheumatoid arthritis; and when the pain is very bad and his father is lovingly attending to her, Ned must tiptoe around the house. He feels her pain "as if his own bones were turning into water." For Ned's birthday his uncle gives him an air rifle. But his father forbids him to use it, and it is put away in the attic. Ned feels he must try it just once. That night he takes the gun, and, outside in the moonlight, he shoots at something that moves, a "dark shadow." Some time later, when he's working for a neighbor, old Mr. Scully, they notice a wild cat in the yard, and they see that there's something wrong with it.

> The cat was as gray as a mole and its fur was matted. As it peered toward the house, it shook its head constantly as though to clear away something that made seeing difficult.
>
> "What's the matter with him?" Ned asked.
>
> "Hunger," replied Mr. Scully. "No. Wait a minute. There is something wrong."
>
> "One of its eyes is shut tight."
>
> The cat came closer to the house.
>
> "The eye isn't there," Ned said. "There's just a little hole." He felt a touch of fear.
>
> Mr. Scully pressed against the counter. Ned could feel his breath.
>
> "You're right." Mr. Scully said. "The cold does that to them sometimes, and he looks big enough to have been born last year. Or else someone used him for target practice. A boy would do that. A living target is more interesting than a tin can." [p. 66]

> "Hunting will be hard for him now," [Mr. Scully said]. "These cats live pretty good off rodents until the ground freezes over. I'll keep food out for him. Maybe he'll manage."

Ned didn't think he would. He'd seen the gap, the dried blood, the little worm of mucus in the corner next to the cat's nose where the eye had been. [p. 70]

Ned feels responsible for the cat's pain. His guilty secret weighs on him and poisons everything. He feels that it separates him from his parents, who believe he is loving and good.

Eckert, Allan. *Incident at Hawk's Hill*. Little, Brown, 1971. Adult; gr. 6 up

Ben is a strange, shy little boy, awkward with people. But farm and wild animals on the Canadian prairie come to him; he has an uncanny ability to mimic their movements and sounds.

One day he sees a hawk tearing at a mouse. He finds the mouse's nest and four tiny baby mice that will die. Suddenly he finds himself face to face with an enormous female badger. It could be ferocious. Knowing that the tiny mice will die anyway, should he let the badger have them?

> Better a swift, merciful death than the lingering one of starvation. It was with compassion and vague regret then, rather than with maliciousness and cruelty, that he slowly and carefully moved his free hand to the other and extracted one of the mice. Between his thumb and forefinger he pinched the tiny head and felt the little animal go limp. It was the first time he had ever deliberately killed anything, but he did not dwell on the thought. Slowly, still staying on his stomach, he stretched his arm out toward the badger, the dead baby mouse dangling from his fingers. [p. 48]

The badger takes it. Then Ben kills another mouse and feeds it to the badger. With each mouse the badger gets closer, until she takes the last one from his hand and licks him and lets him touch her.

Later the badger is caught in a vicious trap. She jerks back, but part of her foot is caught. Nearby she hears the cries of her hungry pups, but she can't get free. After four agonizing days she finally wrenches free, losing two toes. But her pups are dead.

Ben wanders away from home. Lost in a storm, he shelters in a burrow, the burrow of that badger to whom he fed the mice. And she cares for him as if he were her child; for two months they live together until Ben's brother finds him.

Any of the passages mentioned make dramatic read-alouds, or read the scene (p. 104) where boy and badger share a raw prairie chicken. You can tell so much of the story because the plot is not important here—in fact you can summarize it before you begin. The whole book makes a wonderful junior high read-aloud. It has exquisite drawings by John Schoenherr of Ben, the animals, and the prairie.

Herriot, James. *All Creatures Great and Small.* St. Martin's, 1972. Adult; gr. 7 up

Dr. James Herriot is a country vet in Yorkshire, England, who writes about his work with love and gentle humor. He combines the animal and human interest with clinical detail. As the book begins, he is fresh out of school, trying to deliver a calf that is turned the wrong way inside the mother.

"They didn't say anything about this in the books," he thinks, as he lies "face down on the cobbled floor in a pool of nameless muck, my arm deep inside the straining cow."

> My mind went back to that picture in the obstetrics book. A cow standing in the middle of a gleaming floor while a sleek veterinary surgeon in a spotless parturition overall inserted his arm to a polite distance. He was relaxed and smiling, the farmer and his helpers were smiling, even the cow was smiling. There was no dirt or blood or sweat anywhere. [p. 1]

He's been trying for two hours to get a looped rope round the calf's jaw. He's watched by a "long, sad, silent" farmer and his "long, sad, silent" gloomy son; and worst of all by Uncle, a chirpy know-it-all who kibbitzes all the time, telling Herriot what an expert vet would do.

Any number of the self-contained incidents in this book and its three sequels make comic and/or poignant booktalks that appeal to a wide age range.

Bond, Nancy. *A Place to Come Back To.* Atheneum/Margaret K. McElderry, 1984. YA; gr. 6–10

Charlotte, the New England girl in *A Place to Come Back To*, doesn't particularly like animals. This is how she thinks about Amos, the beloved dog of her friend Oliver:

> She wasn't overly fond of animals, though she tolerated them; she lived quite amicably with her brother Eliot's cats, but they were independent, relatively undemanding creatures. Amos was the most peculiar dog she had ever seen. He was gray and woolly, with a long, blunt-nosed, homely head. He looked as if he'd been put together from several different-sized, do-it-yourself dog kits. He was big, but his front legs appeared to be shorter than his hind legs; he gave the impression of going downhill, whether walking, shambling, or hurtling. He had a long tail, rather sparsely covered with coarse gray hair, as if whoever had assembled him had begun to run short of covering at the hind end and had stretched what was left as far as possible.
>
> He had been thrown out of a car . . . .
>
> He was a very moist dog, always licking exposed skin wherever he could find it, ingratiating, rather simple, annoyingly eager to please. [pp. 12–13]

This dog, Amos, is very important to Oliver, who is alone and unwanted in his family. Oliver and Charlotte have been friends since childhood, but now their relationship is changing. Oliver loves Charlotte and needs her desperately, but it's hard for them to reach out to each other. They can't say what they feel. They don't know what they feel. The dog Amos plays a part in bringing them together.

Lawrence, D. H. "Snake." 1923. From *The Complete Poems of D. H. Lawrence,* Viking. Adult; gr. 7 up

This excerpt from "Snake" makes a dramatic read-aloud, moving from the immediacy of a man's encounter with a very real snake to his thoughts about what society has taught him to fear.

> A snake came to my water-trough
> On a hot, hot day, and I in pyjamas for the heat,
> To drink there.
>
> In the deep, strange-scented shade of the great dark carob-tree
> I came down the steps with my pitcher
> And must wait, must stand and wait, for there he was at the trough
>   before me.
>
> He reached down from a fissure in the earth-wall in the gloom
> And trailed his yellow-brown slackness soft-bellied down, over the edge
>   of the stone trough
> And rested his throat upon the stone bottom,
> And where the water had dripped from the tap, in a small clearness,
> He sipped with his straight mouth,
> Softly drank through his straight gums, into his slack long body,
> Silently.
>
> Someone was before me at my water-trough,
> And I, like a second comer, waiting.
>
> He lifted his head from his drinking, as cattle do,
> And looked at me vaguely, as drinking cattle do,
> And flickered his two-forked tongue from his lips, and mused a moment,
> And stooped and drank a little more,
> Being earth-brown, earth-golden from the burning bowels of the earth
> On the day of Sicilian July, with Etna smoking.
>
> The voice of my education said to me
> He must be killed.
> For in Sicily the black, black snakes are innocent, the gold are
>   venomous.
> And voices in me said, If you were a man
> You would take a stick and break him now, and finish him off.

But must I confess how I liked him,
How glad I was he had come like a guest in quiet, to drink at my water-
trough
And depart peaceful, pacified, and thankless,
Into the burning bowels of this earth?

Was it cowardice, that I dared not kill him?
Was it perversity, that I longed to talk to him?
Was it humility, to feel so honoured?
I felt so honoured.

And yet those voices:
If you were not afraid, you would kill him!

And truly I was afraid, I was most afraid,
But even so, honoured still more
That he should seek my hospitality
From out the dark door of the secret earth.

MORE ANIMALS

Alexander, Lloyd. *The Kestrel.* Dutton, 1982. CH/YA; gr. 5–9
    Fighting for his queen, who is also the woman he loves, and enraged
by the death of his friend, young Theo becomes a great leader in battle.
They call him the Kestrel-hawk for his fierceness, and he turns into a
bloodthirsty animal. Then a crisis shocks him out of the mindless
brutality he thought was honor.

Bell, Clare. *Ratha's Creature.* Atheneum/Margaret K. McElderry, 1983. YA;
    gr. 7 up
    Millions of years ago, in a society of intelligent wild cats, Ratha, a
beautiful young cat, accidentally learns to tame fire, and finds herself
locked in a power struggle with the pack leader. (See Sally Estes's review
in *Booklist* (79:956, March 15, 1983), for a discussion of how Bell captures
both Ratha's intelligence and her feline nature.)

Burnford, Sheila. *The Incredible Journey.* Little, Brown, 1961. Adult classic;
    gr. 5 up
    In a realistic animal survival-adventure story, three pets—a Lab-
rador retriever, an old bull terrier, and a Siamese cat—make their way
back to their home through 250 miles of the Canadian wilderness.

Garner, Alan. *The Weirdstone of Brisingamen.* Collins, 1960; Walck, 1969.
    CH/YA; gr. 5–9
    A terrifying and beautiful fantasy in which (as in the novels of Susan

Cooper) contemporary young people become involved in a fight with creatures of ancient evil that would rule the world. Read aloud from scenes like the one where the carrion crow watching Susan and Colin on the lonely hills gives a loud, sharp croak, and a score of strange figures rise out of the shadows (ch. 3).

Lawick-Goodall, Jane van. *In the Shadow of Man*. Houghton, 1971. Adult; gr. 7 up

In easy anecdotal style, and with superb photos by her husband, Hugo, Goodall describes her ten-year field study of a chimpanzee community in Tanzania. She makes you see individual chimpanzee personalities while she discusses important scientific findings about chimpanzee toolmaking, family organization, sex, and death.

Dian Fossey's *Gorillas in the Mist* (Houghton, 1983) describes a similar study of the African mountain gorilla.

LeVert, John. *The Flight of the Cassowary*. Atlantic, 1986. YA; gr. 8–10

Fascinated with animal behavior, John sees himself and other humans behaving like animals everywhere, from the classroom and the football field to the family dinner table, and in sudden, intense moments he feels that he becomes a particular animal. Read from one of the funny scenes where he sees people around him as animals. I like the laid-back conversation he has with a neighborhood dog about protecting territory. (See Patty Campbell's "Young Adult Perplex" column in *Wilson Library Bulletin,* April, 1986, for a sensitive appreciation of this book.)

Strieber, Whitley. *Wolf of Shadows*. Sierra Club/Knopf, 1985. CH/YA; gr. 5–9

A wolf tells this story, which is set after a nuclear holocaust. A woman and her daughter become part of his wolf pack as he leads them on a 700-mile journey south from Minnesota through the ice, darkness, and death of nuclear winter.

Swarthout, Glendon. *Bless the Beasts and Children*. Doubleday, 1970. Adult; gr. 8 up

A group of unhappy teenage boys, the outsiders at a summer camp, find self-respect and freedom when they work together to free a herd of buffalo about to be brutally slaughtered.

6 Survival

London, Jack. "Love of Life"
Speare, Elizabeth. *The Sign of the Beaver*
Burnford, Sheila. *The Incredible Journey*
Highwater, Jamake. *Ceremony of Innocence*
Brooks, Bruce. *The Moves Make the Man*
Peck, Richard. *Remembering the Good Times*
Tevis, Walter. *The Queen's Gambit*
Oneal, Zibby. *In Summer Light*
Orlev, Uri. *Island on Bird Street*
Hamilton, Virginia. *The People Could Fly*

The theme survival encompasses many kinds of struggle, from wilderness adventure and escape from slavery, to family conflict and teenage suicide.

London, Jack. "Love of Life." 1905. From *Great Short Works of Jack London*.
Harper Perennial Classic, 1965. Adult classic; gr. 7 up
Two heavily burdened, exhausted men limp painfully through the Alaskan wilderness. They haven't eaten for two days and they are out of ammunition. They are trying to reach their cache of food and ammunition and the canoe that will take them back to civilization. Suddenly the man behind slips and sprains his ankle. He calls out in pain to the man in front—who continues straight on without looking back. Alone and desolate, the lame man drags himself through the gray northern summer landscape: "No trees, no shrubs, no grasses," just moss, some water, swirling fog. He counts his matches, then panics and counts them again (p. 329).
Chilled and sickened by a mixture of snow and rain, he goes "hunger

mad." He has hallucinations. Then he loses his sense of hunger and forces himself to eat tiny fish, odd berries, the little he can scrounge, and that makes him hungry again. There are wolves, but they have caribou to hunt, and they don't worry him. He staggers on; then, his feet like raw meat, he drags himself, crawling on his hands and knees.

He becomes aware of a coughing, snuffling sound. A sick wolf is near him, trailing him with feeble and uncertain steps, unable to hunt, and "he knew the sick wolf clung to the sick man's trail in the hope that the man would die first." He finds the body of the friend who abandoned him, the bones picked clean. As he crawls on, his knees become raw like his feet, and the wolf licks hungrily at the bloody trail. The man sees a ship in the distance, but he lacks the strength to crawl the last few miles. Exhausted, but desperate to live, almost unconscious, he hears the sick wolf's wheezing breath coming slowly nearer.

> The patience of the wolf was terrible. The man's patience was no less terrible. For half a day he lay motionless, fighting off unconsciousness and waiting for the thing that was to feed upon him and upon which he wished to feed. [p. 345]

He feels the wolf's tongue along his hand.

> He waited. The fangs pressed softly; the pressure increased; the wolf was exerting its last strength in an effort to sink teeth in the food for which it had waited so long. But the man had waited long, and the lacerated hand closed on the jaw. Slowly, while the wolf struggled feebly and the hand clutched feebly, the other hand crept across to a grip. Five minutes later the whole weight of the man's body was on top of the wolf. The hands had not sufficient strength to choke the wolf, but the face of the man was pressed close to the throat of the wolf and the mouth of the man was full of hair. At the end of half an hour the man was aware of a warm trickle in his throat. It was not pleasant. It was like molten lead being forced into his stomach, and it was forced by his will alone. Later the man rolled over on his back and slept. [p. 345]

And he lives.

Many of London's great stories are about one person alone in the savage northern wilderness. He wrote about wolves and fierce dogs and the basic human needs for food and warmth. Other short stories are "To Build a Fire," and "The Law of Life." Two novels about dogs are *White Fang* and *The Call of the Wild*.

This is a very long booktalk. Sometimes I describe the dramatic opening of the injured man abandoned and leave the audience to read on. But with short stories, it's sometimes effective to tell the whole story as an introduction to the author's work.

After a long booktalk like this, use several short ones to vary the pace.

Speare, Elizabeth George. *The Sign of the Beaver*. Houghton, 1983. CH/YA;
gr. 5–8

Matt (age twelve) is left alone to guard the family's newly built cabin
in the Maine wilderness in early colonial times. His father will be gone
about six weeks, fetching Matt's mother and sister and the new baby from
Massachusetts. A stranger steals Matt's gun, leaving him with no protec-
tion and no way to find meat. A bear gets into his flour. Climbing a tree for
some honey, he is attacked by a swarm of bees. He is saved by an old Indian man, Saknis, and his grandson, Attean. The old man nurses Matt and
asks him to teach Attean to read: Saknis wants Attean to be able to understand the white man and his treaties. Neither boy is at all keen—in fact Attean is angry and sullen. But Attean enjoys Matt's beloved book, *Robinson
Crusoe*. Slowly friendship grows between them, and as Attean teaches
Matt to trap animals and survive in the wilderness, Matt realizes that the
story, *Robinson Crusoe*, had it all wrong: it is the native Friday who would
have known his way around and led the white man shipwrecked on
the island.

The building up of concrete detail is effective; and a good episode to
tell is the attack of the bees in chapter 5. Even young junior high readers
are stimulated by rethinking the Robinson Crusoe myth. But the book has
the elemental appeal of survival, adventure, and friendship; and an effective booktalk could just state the basic situation—boy alone in the wilderness who makes contact with the Indians.

Burnford, Sheila. *The Incredible Journey*. Little, Brown, 1961. Adult classic;
gr. 5 up

Three pets who have always lived happily together—a red-gold Labrador retriever, an old bull terrier, and a Siamese cat—have been moved
far from their home while their owner is away overseas. But the Labrador
wants to go home; and led by him, they make their way back 250 miles
through the Canadian wilderness. Alone they wouldn't have made it, but
they survive together. The Labrador leads. The cat hunts—he is closest to
the wild—yet he can't cross water. The old terrier finds the going very difficult, but he comes into his own in a fight, when a collie dog attacks them.
The story doesn't give the animals human ideas and feelings. Each animal
is a distinctive character, and shows courage, love, and endurance, but is
always true to its animal nature.

This is an extremely popular animal survival-adventure. Young people
appreciate being told that there is no cutesy anthropomorphism. Of
course this also integrates well with the themes of journeys or friendship.

Highwater, Jamake. *Ceremony of Innocence*. Harper, 1985. YA; gr. 8
up

The Indian woman Amana endures alone among strangers in Highwater's *Ceremony of Innocence,* which is based on the grim fate of the northern plains Indians as the whites take over their land. Amana struggles bitterly as she witnesses the near destruction of her people and their way of life and watches her daughter grow up without identity "with dreams that are too small to come true." There are scenes of intense anguish, as when the broken and hungry tribal elders, "prisoners in their own land," are forced to lead their people to the wasteland of the reservation:

> "We have come to escort you and your people to the reservation," the Lieutenant said.
> "On the reservation there is no game. We would have nothing to eat," the chief murmured as he stood weak with hunger and bent with humiliation.
> "I am instructed to escort you to your reservation. And I am instructed to use force if necessary to carry out my orders," the soldier declared in a toneless voice.
> "We must talk among ourselves," Red Crow said, gesturing to the elders who gathered wearily around the chief.
> A council was held. It was not a great meeting of great men as these councils once had been. The elders were sad. They came together at the command of the soldiers; and they spoke not as leaders but as prisoners in their own land. [p. 74]

And when they get there:

> It was a place of terrible poverty. Nowhere was there the track of an animal. There was nothing but wind and snow. [p. 76]

I would show the misery but also the endurance. This is fine historical fiction.

Brooks, Bruce. *The Moves Make the Man.* Harper, 1984. YA; gr. 8 up
Jerome Foxworthy knows the moves you need to survive—in basketball and with people. Brilliant academically, he is also savvy about the real world. Strengthened by his loving home, he can withstand the racism he encounters in school and society. His white friend, Bix, is emotionally fragile, living with a stepfather he hates, his mother in a mental institution. Jerome teaches Bix to play basketball, and athletic Bix learns the skills of the game fast. What he won't learn, absolutely refuses to learn, are the fake moves:

> No fakes, he said.
> Come on, man! What's the big deal? You can't be any kind of a hoops player without fakes! Why are you—
> NO, he said, booming it. I stopped and watched him. His eyes were getting

bad now. No fakes, no tricks, he said. I don't need them. I won't use them.

Then you won't play basketball for beans, I said.

Yes I will, he said. His eyes got wide again but this time they were hot inside and my stomach tightened up at the weirdness coming on. Oh, I will play all right. I will play better than anybody who DOES use lies.

Oh jeez, I said, smacking the ball down and letting it bounce high over my head, jeez here we are with this lie crap again. Fakes are lies, cracker pies are lies, jokes are lies, everything is a lie to you that is just a move to everybody else. What is your problem, dude?

Never mind my problem, he said. Whatever my problem is, it ain't lying. I do not spend all my time teaching my body to trick people like you do. Part of the game, you tell me. Well, it that's so, this game is not a game at all. [p. 179]

But Bix challenges his stepfather in a game that Bix has to win.

This story makes you ask yourself: is Bix stupid, pure, victim, bad? Do we need to wear masks to survive?

(Some of this booktalk is based on Denise Wilms's review that appeared in *Booklist* (81:782, February 1, 1985).)

Peck, Richard. *Remembering the Good Times.* Delacorte, 1985. YA; gr. 7–10

Buck remembers his friendship with Trav and how they both loved the same girl, their classmate Kate. Trav is brilliant, intense, driven—suicidal; unable to accept himself or the loving, perfectionist parents he so resembles. School fails him; it is a wasteland without stimulation or meaning—pointless classes, blank faces, suppressed violence. He turns the violence in on himself.

This book is about personal tragedy; it is also a witty commentary on the way we live now. There's Rusty, new to their Midwest school:

"Because I'm from California," she said, "so I'm flexible." The three friends ask her what schools are like in California:

We got to talking about school things. Trav brought up the subject. "What are California schools like?"

Rusty leaned back in the chair. "Basically optional," she said. "You've got your burnouts and your Vals and your heads and your modified heads and your granola people. You've got your Souls, your Anglos, your low-riders, your boat people. Everybody's in little boxes." She paused. "Like here, come to think about it, but the climate's better."

"I meant academically," Trav said.

Rusty thought about that—thought about Trav, maybe.

"It's there if you want it, but most people are majoring in personal image. Basically, it's too easy. Even with a room-temperature IQ you can pull down a couple of A's for the report card. That's enough to mellow out most parents. So then you think, Why worry?"

"Like here," Trav said. "Like everywhere." [p. 112]

Tevis, Walter. *The Queen's Gambit*. Random, 1983. Adult; gr. 8 up

Beth grows up in a repressive children's home where residents are given daily tranquilizers to keep them quiet. One day when she is eight, she is sent to the basement to clean the blackboard erasers, and she sees the janitor playing a mysterious board game. She badgers him:

> "Will you teach me?"
>
> Mr. Shaibel said nothing, did not even register the question with a movement of his head. Distant voices from above were singing "Bringing in the Sheaves."
>
> She waited for several minutes. Her voice almost broke with the effort of her words, but she pushed them out, anyway: "I want to learn to play chess."
>
> Mr. Shaibel reached out a fat hand to one of the larger black pieces, picked it up deftly by its head and set it down on a square at the other side of the board. He brought the hand back and folded his arms across his chest. He still did not look at Beth. "I don't play strangers."
>
> The flat voice had the effect of a slap in the face. Beth turned and left, walking upstairs with the bad taste in her mouth.
>
> "I'm not a stranger," she said to him two days later. "I live here." Behind her head a small moth circled the bare bulb, and its pale shadow crossed the board at regular intervals. "You can teach me. I already know some of it, from watching."
>
> "Girls don't play chess." Mr. Shaibel's voice was flat. [pp. 7–8]

But she persuades him to teach her. As a little girl, she risks beatings when she steals away secretly to play; by junior high, she is state champion.

The read-aloud communicates the simplicity and tension of Tevis's writing and the power of Beth's obsessive drive.

Oneal, Zibby. *In Summer Light*. Viking Kestrel, 1985. YA; gr. 7 up

High school senior Kate feels defeated: bored, lonely, irritable. Although she's a talented artist, she's given up painting, crushed by her famous and domineering artist father. She used to adore him, but now she's furiously resentful, and her anger is crippling her. Then she falls in love with Ian, a sensitive graduate student working with her father. Read from the scene in which Kate declares her love for Ian:

> She had no preamble. She hadn't tried to think of one. She looked once around the room, so utterly familiar, and then she looked at him and pushed off into thin air.

"Ian," she said, "take me with you to Boston."

This was all she said, but it seemed to take a long time. There were wide spaces between the words, gaps big enough to fall through. The sentence was like a journey undertaken, miles between its beginning and its end, and when it was finished, Kate stared at the floor. All around her there was silence.

When finally she raised her head to look at him, Ian said simply, "Oh, Kate."

His face was expressionless, as blank as any face she had ever seen. She stood waiting, but she saw there was nothing to wait for. Everything she needed to know was written there where nothing was written. It was as if she had entered into a bad old dream.

Ian started to speak. Kate shook her head. "Don't," she said. "You don't have to say anything. I know what you'll say. You're here to do my father's cataloging. That has nothing to do with me."

Her sentence had been the journey, she thought. All the journey that there was going to be. She had put out her hand, and he was moving away. He seemed to be dissolving before her, but it might be, Kate thought, that this was because there were tears in her eyes. [p. 123]

Or you can discuss Kate's love of work. This book tells you about a serious artist: the fierce commitment, the drudgery, the exhilaration. I sometimes read the scene on page 24, where she watches her father's intense struggle with a canvas, or her statement to a rude critic of her father:

"Painting has to do with knocking yourself out day after day trying to get what you want to down on the canvas. Maybe it works and maybe it doesn't, but every day you try. That's what painting is." [p. 146]

It is important not to mislead—this is not a YA romance. The read-aloud will show readers that this is a subtle book, intense but understated. This provides variety within a presentation on survival and gives balance to the action/adventure books. Of course it also integrates well with themes of family and work.

Orlev, Uri. *The Island on Bird Street*. Houghton, 1984. Tr. from Hebrew by Hillel Halkin. CH/YA; gr. 5–9

This Holocaust story is based on the author's own experience as a child in the Warsaw ghetto. The ghetto within the city, where the Jews were forced to live, is almost deserted. Most of the Jews have been taken away to extermination camps. Alex's mother is already gone. One day they come for his father and the few other Jews who are left. Alex escapes through the sacrifice of his father's friend, who tells Alex to hide out in a ruined bombed house in the deserted area and wait for his father's return. It might be a few days, but Alex must wait. "Even if it took a whole month.

Even if it took a whole year." This is the story of how Alex survives, alone in hiding, with only his white mouse for company. He thinks of himself as a Robinson Crusoe on a desert island, foraging for food, using secret passages between the abandoned houses. The physical details are fascinating—how he builds his hideout, what he eats, how he uses the bathroom, how he keeps warm.

And he waits.

Hamilton, Virginia. *The People Could Fly: American Black Folktales*. Knopf, 1985. CH/YA; gr. 5 up

The beautiful title story in this collection is both anguished and hopeful, a fantasy about those who flew away from brutality to freedom, and those who had to stay and who told the story.

> They say the people could fly. Say that long ago in Africa, some of the people knew magic. And they would walk up on the air like climbin up on a gate. And they flew like blackbirds over the fields. Black, shiny wings flappin against the blue up there.
>
> Then, many of the people were captured for Slavery. The ones that could fly shed their wings. They couldn't take their wings across the water on the slave ships. Too crowded, don't you know. [p. 166]

Then, when they came to America:

> The slaves labored in the fields from sunup to sundown. The owner of the slaves callin himself their Master. Say he was a hard lump of clay. A hard, glinty coal. A hard rock pile, wouldn't be moved. His Overseer on horseback pointed out the slaves who were slowin down. So the one called Driver cracked his whip over the slow ones to make them move faster. That whip was a slice-open cut of pain. So they did move faster. Had to. [p. 167]

The story focuses on a young woman Sarah, laboring in the fields with a baby on her back. In her suffering she remembers how to fly—and she and others fly away from brutality to freedom. But some could not fly. They had to stay, and they told and retold the story. Hamilton says of some of them in her note, they "had only their imaginations to set them free."

Blending fantasy and history, this story speaks to all of us about courage in the face of oppression.

Hamilton's dramatically retold American black folktales make fine booktalks for all ages. The large, illustrated format may deter some older readers, though the pictures by Leo and Diane Dillon are splendid. The notes and introduction will certainly draw young adults who are interested in the stories' origins. I talk about Hamilton's introduction, in which she emphasizes the creativity of the slaves whose stories combined their

African heritage with the sorrow of their oppression, as they secretly and symbolically told one another their hopes and fears.

There are many kinds of stories, and I choose whichever one fits my theme. Some combine fun and horror, like the Hairy Man: he was "coarse-hairy all over. His eyes burned red as fire. He had great big teeth, with spit all in his mouth and running down his chin" (p. 91).

There's the true escape narrative "Carrying the Running-Aways" about rowing runaway slaves across the Ohio River: "We were so scared and it was so dark and we knew we could get caught and never get gone" (p. 145). Hamilton's note at the end of the story relates it to her own grandfather's story of escape, told to her by her mother. What better story for a booktalk on survival?

MORE SURVIVAL

Creations: The Quest for Origins in Story and Science. Ed. by Isaac Asimov, George Zebrowski, and Martin Greenberg. Crown, 1983. Adult; gr. 7 up

This anthology of science fiction, science, and myth includes two wonderful time-travel outsider stories.

In "The Doctor" by Theodore L. Thomas a doctor finds himself living half a million years ago in a savage, suspicious community. With his knowledge of modern technology, he tries to set a leg, remove a tooth, and perform a tracheotomy with a sharp flint.

"The Ugly Little Boy" by Isaac Asimov is about a Neanderthal boy who is brought into our time for observation like a laboratory animal.

Finney, Jack. *About Time: Twelve Stories.* Simon & Schuster, 1986. Adult; gr. 7 up

A collection of a great science-fiction writer's time and time-travel stories: quiet, witty, imaginative, romantic. My favorite is "Such Interesting Neighbors," set in the twenty-first century, when time travel is available to the masses, and people use it to escape to their favorite times and places in the history and geography of the world. (Again, thanks to Sally Estes, whose enthusiasm for these stories first made me read them.)

Golding, William. *Lord of the Flies.* Coward, McCann, 1954. Adult classic; gr. 8 up

Marooned on a tropical island, a group of English schoolboys tries to set up an ordered society, but most of them descend into savagery and begin to hunt each other to death.

Graham, Robin and Derek L. T. Gill. *Dove*. Harper/Trophy, 1972. Adult;
gr. 7 up
Dove is the name of the 24-foot sloop on which 16-year-old Graham
sailed on a five-year journey around the world. This is an example of the
many true-adventure books that go well with this theme. Try also *Alive:
The Story of the Andes Survivors* by Piers Paul Read (Harper, 1974); and
Dougal Robertson's *Survive the Savage Sea* (Praeger, 1973).

Green, Hannah. *I Never Promised You a Rose Garden*. Holt, 1964. Adult; gr.
8 up
In an autobiographical novel, Hannah Green (pseudonym for
Joanne Greenberg) describes the struggle of a teenage schizophrenic girl
to leave her private fantasy kingdom. A wise psychiatrist helps her to face
the harsh challenges of the real world.

Guest, Judith. *Ordinary People*. Viking, 1976. Adult; gr. 8 up
Teenage Conrad, home from the hospital after attempting suicide, is
painfully trying to pick up his life again. Feeling a stranger at home and at
school, he faces his fierce feelings with the help of a funny, wise
psychiatrist.

Guy, Rosa. *The Disappearance*. Delacorte, 1979. YA; gr. 7–10
Inner-city teenager Imamu Jones has only his intelligence to save
him. He has been taken into the foster home of the middle-class black
Aimsley family, and they are kind to him. But when their little girl disap-
pears, Imamu must find her—to save himself from being the accused.
This is a fine mystery as well as a book about survival.

Halberstam, David. *The Amateurs*. Morrow, 1985. Adult; gr. 9 up
Excellence in sports requires concentration, commitment, arduous
training. In this nonfictional account of four young men's quest for the
1984 Olympic Gold Medal in rowing, one of the competitors talks about
the pain that has to be endured, in the training and in each race:

> In truth, deep down, he liked this aspect of the sport because it permitted or-
> dinary and not particularly talented young men and women to reach beyond
> themselves. "I think," he once said, "that what I like about it is the chance to
> be a hero." [p. 62]

Hersey, John. *Hiroshima*. Knopf, 1946. Adult classic; gr. 9 up
Hersey focuses on six survivors in a classic account of the ruin
caused by the Bomb.

Lipsyte, Robert. *One Fat Summer*. Harper, 1977. YA; gr. 7–10
Overweight Bobby Marks slims down the summer he is fourteen. He

also sticks to an exhausting job and learns to stand up to his father, his unfair employer, and the local bullies.

In the sequels, *Summer Rules* (1981) and *The Summerboy* (1982), an older, thinner Bobby, pursuing work, girls, and glory, is faced with painful moral choices.

Mandela, Winnie. *Part of My Soul Went with Him*. Ed. Anne Benjamin. Norton, 1985. Adult; gr. 8 up

In her own voice—proud, angry, funny, religious, nonracist—the wife of Nelson Mandela, the imprisoned South African leader, tells her story of brutal persecution by the apartheid regime and heroic resistance by herself and many others.

Sebestyen, Ouida. *Words by Heart*. Atlantic/Little, Brown, 1979. CH/YA; gr. 5–10

In 1910 young Lena Sills and her family are the first blacks to move into a small western town. Some of the whites feel threatened by the Sills and use violence to drive them out. But Lena's father—strong, proud, Christian—refuses to leave and he doesn't believe in violence.

Steinem, Gloria. "Ruth's Song (Because She Could Not Sing It)". From *Outrageous Acts and Everyday Rebellions*. Holt, 1983. Adult; gr. 9 up

Ms. magazine editor Gloria Steinem talks about how she grew up in squalid poverty, caring—alone—for her mentally ill mother. I read aloud some of the brief vignettes of that childhood. The young girl protects herself by imagining that this isn't her mother at all; she has been adopted and one day her real parents will find her. Only much later could she see the sadness and waste of her mother's life and understand that many women shared those patterns. This nonfiction account links directly with novels like Naylor's *The Keeper*, in which teenage Nick copes with his mentally ill father. In fact, Steinem's memoir fits with any writing that deals with what she calls "all our family mysteries."

Zolotow, Charlotte, comp. *Early Sorrow: Ten Stories of Youth*. Harper, 1986. Adult/YA; gr. 8 up

A companion to Zolotow's *An Overpraised Season,* this collection for young adults of high-quality adult short stories deals with the pain of growing up—from first love and sexual awakening to the shock of self-betrayal and parental inadequacy. There is no false nostalgia here, no condescension. These stories' power lies in character and moral conflict, and the sudden stumbling onto adult secrets.

7   The Many Faces of Love

McCullers, Carson. *The Ballad of the Sad Café*
Du Maurier, Daphne. *Rebecca*
Rylant, Cynthia. *A Fine White Dust*
Mahy, Margaret. *The Catalogue of the Universe*
McFadden, Cyra. *Rain or Shine*
Stone, Bruce. *Half Nelson, Full Nelson*
Willard, Nancy. *Things Invisible to See*
Hearne, Betsy. "Love Lines"
Dickens, Charles. *A Christmas Carol*

Love's many faces range from conventional romance to passion and obsession and include gay love, family love, and love of all humanity.

McCullers, Carson. "The Ballad of the Sad Café." 1951. From *The Ballad of
the Sad Café and Other Stories*. Bantam, 1958. Adult classic; gr. 10
up

In a dreary, small southern town, "lonesome, sad, and like a place
that is far off and estranged from all other places in the world", one very
old house is boarded up. In that house, a tragic love triangle was once
acted out. Miss Amelia owned the house. She was rich and harsh, with
the bones and muscles of a man, and solitary. Long ago she had been
married very briefly to Marvin Macy, who was "bold and fearless and
cruel." He loved her wildly, but she hit him if he came near her, and he
left town. Years later a stranger came to town, a small hunchback who
said he was her Cousin Lymon, and Miss Amelia fell in love for the first
time in her life and took him in. Then Marvin Macy returned, on parole
from the penitentiary.

As antidote to formula romance, with mature students, try reading what McCullers says about the solitude and suffering of love. Or use it as contrast to Cathy's statement in *Wuthering Heights* about her total union with Heathcliff.

> First of all, love is a joint experience between two persons—but the fact that it is a joint experience does not mean that it is a similar experience to the two people involved. There are the lover and the beloved, but these two come from different countries. Often the beloved is only a stimulus for all the stored-up love which has lain quiet within the lover for a long time hitherto. And somehow every lover knows this. He feels in his soul that his love is a solitary thing. He comes to know a new, strange loneliness and it is this knowledge which makes him suffer . . . .
> Now the beloved can also be of any description. The most outlandish people can be the stimulus for love. A man may be a doddering great-grandfather and still love only a strange girl he saw in the streets of Cheehaw one afternoon two decades past. The preacher may love a fallen woman. The beloved may be treacherous, greasy-headed, and given to evil habits. Yes, and the lover may see this as clearly as anyone else—but that does not affect the evolution of his love one whit. A most mediocre person can be the object of a love which is wild, extravagant, and beautiful as the poison lilies of the swamp. [p. 26] .

Du Maurier, Daphne. *Rebecca*. 1938. Adult classic; gr. 7 up

Rebecca is a contemporary adult classic very close to *Jane Eyre,* with an obscure, orphaned heroine caught up in mystery and romantic suspense.

A young woman (whose name we never learn) tells her story. Poor, plain, and alone, she works as "companion" to a rich, vulgar society lady. They travel a lot, and when they are staying in a fashionable hotel in Monte Carlo, they meet mysterious Maximilian de Winter, a handsome, rich, brooding Englishman whose wife, Rebecca, has recently died. He likes the girl for her innocence and candor. She loves him passionately, and when, after only a few weeks, he asks her to marry him, she agrees. After the wedding they go back to his great English country house, Manderley. But the new bride feels that she can't measure up to the dazzling first wife, Rebecca. The sinister housekeeper, Mrs. Danvers, bullies the new wife, and talks constantly about Rebecca's poise and beauty. And then a terrible secret is revealed.

Rylant, Cynthia. *A Fine White Dust*. Bradbury, 1986. CH/YA; gr. 5–9

Pete growing up in a small North Carolina town has always been religious, though his parents are not. They accept that he goes to church, but they insist that *they* don't have to choose as he does. The summer after Pete finishes seventh grade an intense revival preacher comes to town, and Pete is born again. He realized he loves the Preacher Man, who seems fierce and mysterious:

"I would have died for him," Pete says. "I just wanted to be with him." When the preacher asks Pete to come away with him and help him preach, Pete knows he must go.

It is very hard for him to leave:

> Leaving home.
>
> You think about it now and then. If you could just get away, you could find what you want. If you could just light out on your own, you'd find out about life. You'd be free.
>
> Thinking about home, that morning, and leaving it behind me . . . I tell you, I didn't know it would be so hard.
>
> You love some things without ever knowing it. I never knew how much I loved the window beside my bed till that morning. Every day of my life I woke up next to that window. [p. 59]

Though Pete loves his home, he packs a bag and arranges to meet the preacher secretly at midnight and go away with him.

This is a fine depiction of obsession—at any age: the way one person can seem to answer all your uncertainties and imperfections. I use this book with Willey's *Finding David Dolores*, which is also about obsessive love.

Mahy, Margaret. *The Catalogue of the Universe.* Atheneum/Margaret K. McElderry, 1986. YA; gr. 8 up

Although Angela has grown up beautiful and confident with her strong, loving unmarried mother, she yearns for the father she's never known. She tracks him down, follows him from afar, stands outside his house, and dreams that she "might turn out to be the daughter he's always longed for." But it doesn't work out like that, and in her pain she reaches out to Tycho, the homely boy who has always loved her. In an intense scene, he squeezes himself into a telephone booth where she is phoning her mother, and half-angrily declares his love for her, while people outside are banging to use the phone:

> "All right!" he said at last, "But I'll tell you two things first. I don't know what's happened, but I do know this—whatever your father thinks—if he *is* your father, that is—your mother loves you." The words were stiff but defiant, as if Tycho knew he were offering yet another piece of unwelcome information. "And I'*m* crazy about you," he added as they stared woodenly at one another. "You're all I think about when you're not there," he went on in a matter-of-fact way, as the banging on the door was repeated, "and you're all I think about when you are. So there!" [p. 99]

Tycho has always shared with Angela his excitement for science and the history of ideas, but he thinks of himself as short and strange looking; and when she tells him she admires his brilliant, searching mind, he replies (only half-joking): "I'd rather be tall." This is a funny, tender, and passionate love story about the thrill of real love and the search for ideas that include science and mystery.

McFadden, Cyra. *Rain or Shine*. Knopf, 1986. Adult; gr. 8 up

Cyra McFadden could never please her father—as a child or an adult. In her frank, fast-talking memoir, she describes how she rebelled against a parent who overwhelmed and rejected her. *She* loved *him*. As a child he dazzled her as the "dangerous but dashing" star announcer of the rodeo circuit. After her parents' divorce, she was "manic with joy" whenever he visited her. But she always disappointed him:

> he marched me off instantly to a beauty shop to have a permanent wave, frustrated beyond tolerance that no matter who did what to me, and no matter how much he paid for it, my hair refused to curl. He wanted a daughter who looked like Shirley Temple. Instead, he had a sulky, waiflike child who looked more like Oliver Twist. [p. 5]

Stone, Bruce. *Half Nelson, Full Nelson*. Harper, 1986. YA; gr. 7–10

Sixteen-year-old Nelson loves his family, and he's trying to keep them together in a tacky Florida trailer park. His 270-pound father dreams of making it in big-time wrestling as the wild Gator Man. He brags to his wrestling opponents in dusty small-town halls:

> "The Florentine is a woman, a weak-kneed, chicken-hearted, drooling greaseball who isn't man enough to polish my boots with his miserable tongue. He is trash, he is scum, he is a boil on the armpit of the universe, the ugliest man to ever climb into the ring with the divinely gorgeous Gator Man. And after today he will be even uglier. I will rearrange his face to look like a bowl of last year's tuna salad. I will tie his legs into granny knots and braid his plug-ugly fingers like rope. I will use his eyes for marbles and bite off his nose and spit it back in his face. I will grab that whiny moronic son of a pencil-necked geek by his ears and snap his little pinhead right off his shoulders just like this . . . ." [p. 105]

But his wife wants a civilized life, and she leaves him, taking with her Nelson's little sister. Nelson is determined to reunite his family. He is helped by Heidi, whose sexy, bold manner hides her need. When the sheriff catches Heidi and Nelson on the road, Heidi makes up a sob story that parodies the soaps:

> "Oh, but sheriff, Nelson and I are so truly and deeply in love, it's like these laws are just made up to ruin our lives," Heidi moaned. She scraped her chair across the floor to mine and took my hand to demonstrate the total sincerity of our young love. "Everyone told us to wait until we graduated, but we just *knew* we were doing the right thing. It was like a message from God, the very day my daddy's body rejected a heart transplant." [p. 116]

Young adults like this book for its comedy and for the ongoing tension between real and fake togetherness and individuality. It is a fine example of a "boy's book" that deals with feelings: Nelson becomes the strong, nurturing center for his family and for Heidi.

Willard, Nancy. *Things Invisible to See*. Knopf, 1984. Adult; gr. 8 up

Clare has secretly loved Ben from afar for a long time, but he's never noticed her. When she sees him at school:

> the sight of him made her tremble. She learned his schedule and looked forward to the few minutes between classes when their paths crossed. She watched him in the cafeteria and remembered what he ate and what he left untouched. She memorized his clothes and fell in love with the way he rolled up his shirt sleeves. Saturdays she watched him play, glad that he did not notice her in the stands. [pp. 60–61]

Ben is champion pitcher in his Ann Arbor high school. Fooling with his friends one night in the park, he hits a ball into the darkness. It accidentally hits Clare on the head, paralyzing her. He comes to visit her out of guilt, but he falls in love with her. Magic also makes things happen in this book. Ben has an evil twin who makes a pact with Death to injure Ben; and in an exciting game the Lord of the Universe and Death play ball.

While a booktalk should not tell too much, it would be misleading to present this book as only a realistic love story or as a sports story. You have to show that there's fantasy, too.

Hearne, Betsy. *Love Lines: Poetry in Person*. Margaret K. McElderry Books, 1987. YA; gr. 8 up

Love Lines

Sometimes love rhymes.
The lines in your face and hands
rhyme with mine, the lines
of our bodies easily entwine,
the lines of our minds fine-tuned
to similar rhythms.

In time

you have lined the space of my living like
a string sculpture infinitely extended
a design that defines our space with
gracious whorls and swirls and spheres of
shining strands soft-spun, silken lariats
that sail across skies, catch clouds on the fly,
a magical rope that unbinds and sets free,
yet doubles as a life line on the sea.

> Our feats are not lettered in epics—
> love is not metered in regular beats,
> but when it's refined,
> sometimes love rhymes.

This is the title poem from a collection by Betsy Hearne. Young people would also respond to her introduction about the connections between love and poetry (see above), and especially her comparison with song:

> Sometimes, when a song exactly suits what you're feeling, you want to listen to it over and over instead of hearing other songs. It may be simple, but surprisingly apt. Poetry is the same way. Sometimes you want to repeat the same lines instead of moving into other moods and tempos. If only one of these poems touches you in that way, it will last you a long time, exactly like someone you love.

Dickens, Charles. *A Christmas Carol*, 1843; Penguin, 1971. Adult classic; gr. 6 up

Scrooge needs to be taught about love. He is a cold, tight-fisted, mean, grasping old sinner. "Hard and sharp as flint . . . secret, and self-contained, and solitary as an oyster" (p. 46). On Christmas Eve he sits busy in his counting house. Christmas to him is a foolish sham. His nephew comes to wish him merry Christmas. "Humbug!" says Scrooge . . . "Merry Christmas! Out upon Merry Christmas . . . . If I could work my will . . . every idiot who goes about with 'Merry Christmas' on his lips should be boiled with his own pudding, and buried with a stake of holly through his heart" (p. 48). Two gentlemen come to ask him to help the poor: "Are there no prisons?" (p. 51) answers Scrooge, and refuses to give a penny.

It's a cold, dark, foggy night. As he comes home, the large knocker on his front door becomes for an instant the face of his business partner, Marley, who died in that house seven years ago that very night. "Humbug!" says Scrooge and enters the dark house. But he is frightened enough to check everywhere: "Nobody under the bed; nobody in the closet; nobody in his dressing-gown, which was hanging up in a suspicious attitude against the wall" (p. 56). He double locks the door and settles down before the fire. Then he hears a clanking noise, deep down below in the cellar; as if some person were dragging a heavy chain. . . .

You can stop there or go on to read from and tell the scene between Scrooge and the ghost—a superb combination of horror and humor, with vivid characterization and the clear message of love for humanity. Even if you don't read much of it aloud, read it to yourself before the booktalk; soak up as much of the tone and detail as you can.

MORE LOVE

Brontë, Charlotte. *Jane Eyre*. 1847. Adult classic; gr. 7 up
Orphaned and abused as a child, Jane grows fighting to believe in herself, small, plain, and poor as she is. She gets a job as governess in a rich great house called Thornfield, and she falls in love with its brooding, passionate master, Mr. Rochester. But his house hides an agonizing secret.

Crutcher, Chris. *Running Loose*. Greenwillow, 1983. YA; gr. 7–10
High school senior Louie Banks loses his place on the football team for his antiracist stand, and he learns about love, sex, and loss in his deepening relationship with his girlfriend, Becky.

Emecheta, Buchi. *The Bride Price*. Braziller, 1976. Adult; gr. 9 up
The tragic story of a modern Nigerian girl, Akuk-nna, who rebels against the traditional marriage customs and elopes with the schoolmaster she loves.

Endo, Shusaku. *When I Whistle*. Taplinger, 1979. Adult; gr. 9 up
As he watches his son sell himself for success, a father remembers how he and a close friend loved the same girl in pre-World War II Japan.

Garden, Nancy. *Annie on My Mind*. Farrar, 1982. YA; gr. 8–12
A romantic story about two seniors in high school, Liza and Annie, who find that they are physically attracted to each other and deeply in love.

Graber, Richard. *Doc*. Harper, 1986. YA; gr. 7–12
Teenager Brad can't bear to watch his beloved grandfather degenerate with Alzheimer's disease—a candid, poignant story that celebrates the loving bonds of family and community.

Jones, Diana Wynne. *Howl's Moving Castle*. Greenwillow, 1986. YA; gr. 6 up
Sophie knows that, according to fairy-tale convention, as the eldest she's expected to fail first and worst when she sets out to seek her fortune, so she doesn't even try—until a spell impels her to Wizard Howl's magic castle, where she finds love, adventure, and community.

Kellogg, Marjorie. *Tell Me That You Love Me, Junie Moon*. Farrar, 1968. Adult; gr. 9 up
A funny poignant story of three physically disabled young people—Junie Moon, disfigured by an acid attack; Arthur, victim of a progressive

neurological disease; and Warren, a paraplegic—who set up housekeeping together.

McKinley, Robin. *Beauty: A Retelling of the Story of Beauty and the Beast.* Harper, 1978. CH/YA; gr. 5 up
Like a fantasy novel, this retelling of the fairy tale describes how brave, studious Beauty is forced to come to the Beast's great castle and how she frees him from his hideous enchantment through the power of her love. For a talk on love, I focus on Beauty. For a talk on outsiders, I focus on the Beast.

Magorian, Michelle. *Good Night, Mr. Tom.* Harper, 1982. CH/YA; gr. 6–9
Nine-year-old Willie, abused by his mother, retreats in terror when he is evacuated to the countryside from London during World War II. But the love of Tom, the feisty old man with whom Willie is lodged, allows him to grow strong.
I use the scene when Tom picks up the poker for the fire and Willie faints, thinking that he's going to be attacked with it.

Mazer, Harry. *I Love You, Stupid!* Crowell, 1981. YA; gr. 7–10
In a funny, honest story about loving the girl next door, awkward high school senior Marcus, a virgin obsessed with girls, confides in his good friend, Wendy. They decide to have sex, and he discovers that he loves her, and that lust and liking need not be separate.

Peck, Richard. *Father Figure.* Viking, 1978. YA; gr. 7–10
Jim, seventeen, has always fathered his younger brother until, on the death of their mother, their father returns. Then Jim must compete, not just for the father role, but also for the woman he and his father both love.

Pei, Lowry. *Family Resemblances.* Random, 1986. Adult/YA; gr. 9 up
Teenage Karen learns from her unconventional aunt and from her own intimate experience about some sad secrets of adult passion and uncertainty.

Peyton, K. M. *Flambards.* World, 1968. CH/YA; gr. 6 up
The first of four English romantic novels about orphaned Christina Parsons. The series begins in the Edwardian period and includes World War I and its aftermath.

Roth, Philip. *Goodbye, Columbus.* Houghton, 1959. Adult; gr. 10 up
A poor, young Jewish librarian has a passionate affair with a beautiful girl whose newly rich family has recently moved to the suburbs. A sharp, funny novella.

Vonnegut, Kurt. *Welcome to the Monkey House*. Delta/Seymour Lawrence, 1968. Adult; gr. 9 up

This collection of short pieces contains two funny love stories. "Long Walk to Forever" is a courting story about two twenty-year-olds. It is told almost entirely in dialogue with comic repetition, and it has excellent passages for reading aloud.

"Who Am I This Time?" is about painfully shy Harry Nash, a hardware-store clerk, who can barely say a word to a girl. But he's a great actor and is transformed on stage. In the town's amateur theatrical society's perform-ance of *A Streetcar Named Desire,* he plays the sexy, macho Marlon Brando part, "huge and handsome and conceited and cruel." His co-star falls in love with him; but how to reach him off-stage and without a script?

Walsh, Jill Paton. *Fireweed*. Farrar, 1969. YA; gr. 7–10

Two teenagers find each other when they refuse to evacuate from London during the World War II blitz.

8   The Many Faces of Terror

Cross, Gillian. *On the Edge*
Bess, Clayton. *Story for a Black Night*
Preussler, Otfried. *The Satanic Mill*
Dickens, Charles. *Great Expectations*
Kerr, M. E. *Gentlehands*
Michaels, Barbara. *Be Buried in the Rain*
Bodanis, David. *The Secret House*
Dahl, Roald. "The Sound Machine"
Orwell, George. *1984*
Blake, William. "An Answer to the Parson"
Naylor, Phyllis Reynolds. *The Keeper*
Fox, Paula. *The Moonlight Man*
Conrad, Pam. *Prairie Songs*

Terror is one of the simplest—and most successful—themes: exciting, intense, and wide-ranging in genre, setting, and mood.

You might want to start with popular thrillers or horror stories; if you like these books, you can use them to establish your shared pleasure with young people in a good story. But don't spend time preparing long talks on the very popular books. Young people don't need you to tell them about the latest Stephen King—they'll read his books anyway—and their teachers will have little reason for inviting you back to their classrooms.

Tell them about other stories that speak of nightmare, dislocation, and dread. Show the terror of a runaway slave; a woman going mad on the desolate prairie; the heroism of a prisoner in South Africa; Dickens's convict rising up at Pip from the graveyard; a teenager with an alcoholic parent; a boy summoned in a dream to work for the devil.

For this chapter I have loosely linked some of the talks in just one of a great variety of possible combinations.

The "More . . . " section is brief here, because in fact almost any intense book can be integrated with this theme.

Cross, Gillian. *On the Edge*. Holiday, 1985. YA/CH; gr. 7–10

Tug has been out running. As he comes back to his London house and unlocks the front door, he feels uneasy: "Dark! The house was too dark. . . . And there was something else . . . . " He stretches out his hand towards the light switch—

> Then everything crashed round him. No light. Instead, from behind, from the other side of the door, a body launched itself. An arm went chokingly round his neck and a hand pressed against his face, forcing a pad over his nostrils. [p. 6]

He wakes up the next day and finds he's being held captive by a strange man and woman in the attic of a remote house on the moor. They tell him they're his mother and father, and they play mind games with him, so that he begins to doubt his own perceptions and his memories. When he sees a girl outside, he screams for help, and the woman he's supposed to call Mother beats him up savagely as if she can't stop. Later Tug says to the man: after what that woman did to me, "You can't still be pretending that you're my parents . . . ."

> "Where do you think most murders happen?" murmured Doyle. "And baby-batterings and granny-bashings and wife-beatings?"
> "But—"
> "Who do you think the best torturers are?" Doyle went on, without letting Tug speak. "Your nearest and dearest, of course. They're the ones you can't leave easily. You care about what they think. And they know where your weak places are. Husbands and wives are bad enough. But mothers and fathers are the worst. You can never get rid of them. They have you when you're young and weak and they've got you for ever."
> It was all said quite mildly, without any venom, while he went on rubbing the gun.

Bess, Clayton. *Story for a Black Night*. Parnassus/Houghton, 1982. CH/YA; gr. 4 up

In modern Liberia one night the electricity fails, and Momo tells a story of his childhood, before modernization and before vaccination had eradicated the terrible plague of smallpox. He lived in a hut in the bush, alone with his mother, his baby sister, and his grandmother—who was blind from smallpox. One dark night, when evil seems all around, there is a knock at the door. Momo and his grandmother beg his mother to ignore the travelers there, sure that they mean trouble. But she insists she must give shelter to the wanderers: a mother, a grandmother, and a baby. In the morning the strangers have gone, abandoning the baby—who is discovered to have smallpox. Momo's grandmother hysterically begs his mother to abandon the sick baby. But she can't. She nurses it. When the nearby town refuses her own children shelter, the whole family becomes infected.

Told in dialect by adult Momo to his son, the story twists and turns, with new discoveries of betrayal and grace until the end. No simple judgments are made, and the story makes you ask yourself: What would I have done? Where is the evil?

(This slim volume is a tale of terror and beauty. The strong story and moral sophistication make it superb YA material. But because it was reviewed as a children's book, even though the recommended grade level is 4-up, it has reached too few young adults. I booktalk it through high school, allowing the story to unfold in all its drama.)

Preussler, Otfried. *The Satanic Mill*. Tr. by Anthea Bell. Macmillan/Collier, 1973. CH/YA; gr. 6–10

(The word *evil* is the unobtrusive link to the preceding book.)

Evil forces compel Krabat, a fourteen-year-old beggar boy in seventeenth century Germany. "Between New Year's Day and Twelfth Night" he has a strange dream.

> There were eleven ravens sitting on a perch, looking at him. He saw an empty place down at the end of the perch, on the left, and then he heard a voice. It was a hoarse voice, and it seemed to be coming out of thin air, from very far away, and it called him by his name, but he did not dare reply. "Krabat!" called the voice a second time, and then a third time—"Krabat!" Then it said, "Come to the mill at Schwarzkollm, and you will not regret it!" At these words the ravens rose from their perch, croaking, "Obey the voice of the Master! Obey!" [p. 4]

He dreams the same dream twice more, and he finds himself following that voice, until he comes to a mill. There he joins eleven others as slaves to a harsh master who practices black magic.

Dickens, Charles. *Great Expectations*. 1861. Adult classic; gr. 8 up

Dickens also writes about young people who are helpless in a world of nightmare terror.

The opening of *Great Expectations* is one of the scariest in all fiction. Orphaned young Pip is crying in the graveyard where his parents and brothers and sisters lie buried, as the light begins to fail and a wind comes up on the marshes. Suddenly a great figure starts up with a shout from among the graves:

"Hold your noise!" cried a terrible voice, as a man started up from among the graves at the side of the church porch. "Keep still, you little devil, or I'll cut your throat!"

A fearful man, all in coarse grey, with a great iron on his leg. A man with no hat, and with broken shoes, and with an old rag tied round his head. A man who had been soaked in water, and smothered in mud, and lamed by stones, and cut by flints, and stung by nettles, and torn by briars; who limped, and shivered, and glared, and growled; and whose teeth chattered in his head, as he seized me by the chin.

"Oh! Don't cut my throat, sir," I pleaded in terror. "Pray don't do it, sir."

"Tell us your name!" said the man. "Quick!"

"Pip, sir."

"Once more," said the man, staring at me. "Give it mouth!"

"Pip. Pip, sir." [ch. 10]

The man is an escaped convict. He frightens Pip into stealing food and a file for him. When he is recaptured, Pip feels for the man's suffering as he is led away by the brutal officials.

Not long after this, Pip is summoned to the house of the great lady of the area, Miss Havisham, and ordered to "play" for her diversion. Miss Havisham is like a crazy witch or a waxwork. Jilted on her wedding day many years ago, she stopped the clocks at the moment she heard the news, and she has never left her rooms since. She trails around in her tattered wedding dress amongst the remains of the wedding feast, on which rats and beetles now feed. She has adopted a beautiful young girl, Estella, to wreak her revenge on men.

On his first visit to that strange house, Miss Havisham orders Pip and Estella to play cards, and he falls in love with Estella and feels her contempt:

Miss Havisham beckoned her to come close, and took up a jewel from the table, and tried its effect upon her fair young bosom and against her pretty brown hair. "Your own, one day, my dear, and you will use it well. Let me see you play cards with this boy."

"With this boy! Why, he is a common labouring-boy!"

I thought I overheard Miss Havisham answer—only it seemed so unlikely, "Well? You can break his heart."

"What do you play, boy?" asked Estella of myself, with the greatest disdain.

"Nothing but Beggar my Neighbour, miss."

"Beggar him," said Miss Havisham to Estella. So we sat down to cards.

Like a corpse in grave-clothes, Miss Havisham watches them play.

"He calls the knaves, jacks, this boy!" said Estella with disdain, before our first game was out. "And what coarse hands he has! And what thick boots!"

I had never thought of being ashamed of my hands before; but I began to consider them a very indifferent pair. Her contempt for me was so strong that it became infectious, and I caught it. [ch. 8]

Hopelessly in love, Pip despises himself and his poor background. Then one day he is mysteriously given money to go to London to be made into a gentleman. He is sure that the money comes from Miss Havisham and that she is preparing him to marry Estella. Then the convict returns . . . .

Kerr, M. E. *Gentlehands*. Harper, 1978. YA; gr. 7–10

In M. E. Kerr's story *Gentlehands,* teenage Buddy, like Pip, is trying to impress a rich girl. Buddy is the son of a policeman in a small seaside town, and he is in love with one of the socially elite summer visitors, Skye Pennington. In a funny family quarrel, which takes place in the bathroom, Buddy's father and mother tell him that they are worried about him, especially because he's suddenly spending all his money on clothes. "She's not our class," Buddy's father tells him. But Buddy likes Skye, and he wants to impress her. He starts taking her to visit his grandfather. Buddy's family has never had much to do with the old man. He lives alone in a big, elegant house with books and paintings and antiques, and Skye is impressed. He knows about opera, and he teaches Buddy to pour wine, and they talk, and Buddy likes his grandfather. Then a shocking secret is revealed that stretches back to World War II and the Holocaust.

Michaels, Barbara. *Be Buried in the Rain*. Atheneum, 1985. Adult; gr. 8 up

(Secrets is the link to the preceding book.)

There are secrets and maybe, ghosts, in the half-ruined mansion in Barbara Michaels's *Be Buried in the Rain,* a pleasantly shivery mixture of horror, mystery, and romance. Medical student Julie, a feisty, independent heroine, and archaeologist Alan, who loves her, are investigating why the skeletons of a young woman and her baby have been found on the southern plantation of Julie's grandmother. Whose skeletons are they? Who dug them up? Julie's evil grandmother now lies bedridden in the house, but there are strange movements and noises late at night. As the mystery unfolds, the most terrifying secrets are Julie's half-forgotten memories of her childhood in that sinister house.

Bodanis, David. *The Secret House*. Simon & Schuster, 1986. Adult; gr. 8 up

The Secret House (title here is the link) is a scientific account of the hidden life in an ordinary home—from the electric force fields in the wall sockets to the armies of bacteria and mites on your face, your robe, the kitchen table. There are things you might not want to know: the ingredients of toothpaste; what happens to your skin when you shave or apply antiperspirant; what the milk in your refrigerator might look like to a miniaturized diver. This is an exciting introduction to the microscopic physical and biological events of daily life: the sense of an invisible seething world is sometimes as scary as science fiction.

Dahl, Roald. "The Sound Machine." 1949. From *Hallucination Orbit: Psychology in Science Fiction*. Ed. Isaac Asimov and others. Farrar, 1983. Adult; gr. 7 up

A clever science-fiction short story describes the terror of a seething hidden world that might just be true.

Roald Dahl's "The Sound Machine" is about an inventor whose machine picks up sounds beyond human hearing. In his backyard, with no one around, just the woman next door picking flowers, he puts on the earphones, switches on the machine, and suddenly hears an agonized scream. He switches off, looks around, but nothing seems to be going on. Again he switches on, and again he suddenly hears a high-pitched scream. Then he asks his neighbor to pick a rose while he has the machine on, and he realizes what is screaming . . . .

In the same short-story collection, Donald Westlake's "The Winner" is a powerful account of personal courage in the face of official brutality.

Orwell, George. *1984*. Harcourt, 1949. Adult classic; gr. 8 up

Terror is official, and brainwashing controls people in Orwell's *1984*. Winston Smith drags himself up the stairs to his dreary apartment. On every landing a poster with an enormous face gazes from the wall. "It was one of those pictures which are so contrived that the eyes follow you about when you move. BIG BROTHER IS WATCHING YOU, the caption beneath it ran" (ch. 1). In the apartment the telescreen is always on, both transmitter and receiver. "You had to live—did live, from habit that became instinct—in the assumption that every sound you made was overheard, and, except in darkness, every movement scrutinized." Winston hates the system, hates Big Brother. He knows that his rebellion puts him in terrible danger and that the Thought Police will find him.

He becomes aware that he is being watched by a dark-haired, beautiful young woman at his office, and he suspects that she may be spying on him. Then one day he leaves his desk at work to go to the washroom. The woman comes toward him in the brightly lit corridor. Her arm is in a sling. She stumbles and falls on her injured arm and cries out in pain. He tries to hold back; he can't stop himself. He takes her free hand and helps

her up. She walks away. The whole incident took place in front of a telescreen. But while he was helping her up "the girl had slipped something
into his hand . . . . It was something small and flat . . . a scrap of paper
folded into a square" (ch. 2). He realizes it has a message on it. But he
can't find the privacy to read it—certainly not in the bathrooms, where
the telescreens are watched continuously. Back at his desk he slips the
paper in with his other work, and he reads what she's written:
"I love you."
Loving intimate relationships are forbidden. They struggle to talk—at
first in shouting crowds where hidden microphones can't spy on them—
and to find private places to meet and make love. But such rebellion cannot be allowed, and their love must be brutally smashed.
I used to stop the booktalk at "I love you." But although this is an entic-
ing point, I decided that it was misleading. You have to show the grim atmosphere and the torture. 1984 is neither a love story, nor an action-
packed thriller. The plot isn't the core of the novel. The interest lies in the
way the society controls its citizens, and in the ideas and phrases like "Big
Brother" and "Doublethink" that have become contemporary myths.

Blake, William. "An Answer to the Parson." ca. 1800. Adult; gr. 6
up
Blake's witty poem rebels against conformity:

> "Why of the sheep do you not learn peace?"
> "Because I don't want you to shear my fleece."

(One place this is quoted is in a wide-ranging anthology of humorous
verse, The Norton Book of Light Verse (1986), edited by Russell Baker.)

Naylor, Phyllis Reynolds. The Keeper. Atheneum, 1986. YA; gr. 7–10
Sometimes the terror you imagine can be as bad as any outside
threat. Nick's father is going crazy, but he won't seek help. He's left his
job, and he paces, paces restlessly around the apartment all day long and
sometimes in the middle of the night. He's terrified that a Communist
conspiracy is out to get him; and he's convinced that there are microphones in the living room, and poison in the food. Nick's mother
wants to keep it a secret. But the boy comes home each day to
mounting tension:

> "Dad, I want to help, if you'd just let me!"
> "I believe you, Nick. I know you would. They just won't allow it, that's
> all."
> "I want you to go see a doctor. Any doctor you like."
> "No! A doctor won't help. They'd pump me full of drugs—get me ad-
> dicted, turn me into a zombie. They've bribed the doctors, Nick."

Nick drew in his breath, held it, then let it out again. "Scratch the doctors," he murmured, and went on back to his room. There was an ache inside him that he couldn't handle, and he pressed his palms against his ears to block out his father's footsteps, pacing the hall. Whatever it was that Jacob feared, the fear itself was real—as excruciating a pain, Nick knew, as he could imagine. How must it feel not to be believed by your own family? To feel that you were about to die, yet the others were going on about their business? No matter how desperately Nick wanted to help, there was a wall between him and his father that he couldn't get around or through or over. [pp. 110–11]

Nick's fear and his humanity—his awareness of his father's suffering—will move young people, as will the author's candor based on her own experience of living with a family member who is mentally ill.

Fox, Paula. *The Moonlight Man*. Bradbury, 1986. YA; gr. 7 up
Catherine comes to know her father's pain in *The Moonlight Man*. "Where was he? Where was her father?" For three weeks of the summer vacation Catherine has been stranded at her boarding school, waiting for her father to come and get her. It's to be their first long time alone together since her parents divorced when she was three, twelve years ago. He finally calls, disarming, apologetic as always; and she crosses on the ferry to meet him in Nova Scotia, where they spend a month in a cottage near the sea.

He has always been an exciting, romantic figure to her, a moonlight man. She hasn't known much about him from their snatched infrequent meetings. But always "Catherine wanted to do what her father wanted her to do." Now she hopes for a "splendid journey."

Two days after her arrival she discovers he's an alcoholic, a shambling monster who terrifies and disgusts her. After a night of drinking, he makes her drive his sodden friends home.

The next morning, bitterly ashamed, he promises to stop drinking and charms her into forgiveness. Alone together, they begin to know each other. Her father cooks and reads aloud; he talks about books he loves and places where he promises to take her. Catherine sees that she astonishes him and that he likes her. They laugh a lot. But in unguarded moments she sees his sadness. He is a failed writer, disappointed, drowning.

And always in the background is the terror of his drinking: the memory of that night and the dread that it could happen again.

Conrad, Pam. *Prairie Songs*. Harper, 1985. CH/YA; gr. 6–12
The lonely prairie was a place of dread for some who could not bear the harshness and isolation of pioneer life.

(Or, another link: there's a different kind of terror alone in the wide wilderness.) In Pam Conrad's *Prairie Songs* the young girl, Louisa, loves the solitude of the wide Nebraskan prairie, and she feels secure in her isolated sod house with her loving pioneer family. But her little brother Lester is shy and fearful, especially since their baby sister died. Louisa looks up to the beautiful, cultured doctor's wife, Emmeline, who comes from New York City, shares her books with Louisa, and teaches her to love poetry. But Emmeline can't adjust to the harsh pioneer life, especially to the loneliness. Through her pregnancy she becomes increasingly fragile and uncontrolled. Then a shock brings on the birth prematurely. Louisa's mother helps the doctor, and the birth is long and excruciating. The baby is born dead. Afterwards Louisa's mother comes home in the middle of the night. "She just came in and stood stone still in the middle of the room." Louisa and Lester hear her sobbing as she tells their father how it was:

> "How is Emmeline?" he asked. "Is she all right now?"
>
> "She's alive. Barely. Half alive, knowing her baby's dead . . . .
>
> "But I held that baby, J.T., and he wouldn't breathe. You have no idea. He just jerked a little, and I tried to keep him warm, give him life, but I couldn't. I couldn't do it." She began to cry.
>
> "Shhhhh, now," Poppa said. "You did all you could."
>
> "Momma?" Lester's whisper seemed to shatter the air in the room, as if he had given away the secret that we were listening. "Momma? The baby died?"
>
> "Yes, sweetheart." She walked slowly to our beds and sat down near Lester. Her hair was down her back, and her face was all swollen. "The baby died. He was just too weak and little to live. Come," she said, drawing back the blankets. "Come let me feel how alive you are."
>
> I sprang up, too, and both Lester and me went into her arms. She was trembling and began to rock us. I felt Poppa gather the blanket up around the three of us, and I closed my eyes. We rocked slowly in big rocking movements, back and forth, as vast as the Milky Way, as wide and as far as the prairie. [pp. 101–2]

At this point you might want to loosen the theme further and lead into books about survival or love or family or outsiders, or into John Donne's famous lines that celebrate the enduring connections between us:

> No man is an island entire of itself; every man is a piece of the continent, a part of the main; . . . any man's death diminishes me, because I am involved in mankind; and therefore never send to know for whom the bell tolls; it tolls for thee.
>
> —Meditation XVII. From *Devotions Upon Emergent Occasions*. 1624.

MORE TERROR

Adams, Douglas. *The Hitchhiker's Guide to the Galaxy.* Harmony, 1980.
  Adult; gr. 8 up
  In a hilarious science-fiction comedy, the first of a trilogy, Englishman Arthur Dent wakes up to find he's hitching through space with a
crew of interstellar explorers, after Earth has been demolished to make
way for an intergalactic speedway.

Demetz, Hana. *The House on Prague Street.* St. Martin's, 1980. Adult;
  gr. 7 up
  An understated autobiographical novel in which half-Jewish
Helene, growing up in Nazi-occupied Czechoslovakia, tries to block out
the terror with the routine of ordinary life, even as she witnesses the suffering and disappearance of her family and friends.

Hamilton, Virginia. *Sweet Whispers, Brother Rush.* Putnam/Philomel, 1982.
  YA; gr. 7–12
  Tree loves her mentally handicapped older brother, Dab; and while
their mother is away working as a nurse, often for days at a time, Tree
cares for Dab. She sees that he eats, that he bathes; sometimes she even
has to remind him to sit down as he paces restlessly. Then Tree sees her
uncle's ghost and he takes her back into the past, where she discovers
harsh secrets about her mother.

Some Things Strange and Sinister. Joan Kahn, comp. Harper, 1973 (Avon/
  Flare). Adult/YA; gr. 7 up
  One of an excellent YA anthology series of high-quality adult horror
stories, with appropriately lurid covers. I usually read and tell one of the
stories (my favorites are John Collier's "Thus I Refute Beelzy" and Guy
de Maupassant's "Nerves"). Then I suggest the audience read the others
for themselves. I always slip in a phrase to say that these are not easy
reading.
  Others in the series include *Some Things Dark and Dangerous* and *Some
Things Fierce and Fatal.*

Schlee, Ann. *Ask Me No Questions.* Holt, 1976. CH/YA; gr. 6–10
  Schlee's novel is based on a real incident in Dickens's time. During a
cholera outbreak in London, Laura is sent to stay with her aunt in a country village. The aunt is cold and repressive. There seem to be secrets
everywhere, especially to do with the mysterious house next door, a kind
of charity school for poor children. Then one day when Laura is in her
aunt's barn, she hears scuffling noises such as rats make. She sees that

some of the pauper children have crept in to steal food from her aunt's pigs. Slowly and quietly the horror of the children's deprivation and abuse unfolds.

Westall, Robert. *The Scarecrows*. Greenwillow, 1981. YA; gr. 7–10
English teenager Simon is terrorized by three scarecrows that seem to come silently closer and closer to his house and to threaten his family, especially his new, hated stepfather.

And almost any book about intense confrontation.

Postscript

An eighth-grade student first introduced me to Jack London's short story "Love of Life." I don't remember the boy's name, but I can still remember where we were standing in the library and hear the excitement in his voice. The story had clearly touched him deeply, changed him. That's what made me read it.

Now that story is part of me. I've never thought about it much. I just know it. And scenes from it flash into my mind at odd times.

I tell people about it: family, friends; I booktalk it to groups and individuals.

The talks in this book are stories I want to share in that way. I hope they will take you to some books you didn't know, that will "wound" you in Kafka's sense and become your own. And that you'll keep combining them with more books that matter to you, so that you create your personal booktalk stories and give them to others for their disturbing pleasure.

Selected Bibliography

Best Books for Young Adults. Chicago: ALA. Annual.

The Best of the Best 1970–1982. Chicago: ALA, 1983.

Bodart, Joni. *Booktalk! 2: Booktalking for All Ages and Audiences*. New York: Wilson, 1985.

Books for the Teen Age. New York: New York Public Library. Annual.

Brodkey, Harold. "Reading, The Most Dangerous Game." *New York Times Book Review* (November 24, 1985), p. 1.

Chelton, Mary K. "Booktalking—You Can Do It." *School Library Journal* 22:39–43 (April 1976).

Cole, Doris M. "The Book Talk." In *Juniorplots* by John Gillespie and Diana Lembo, pp. 1–6. New York: Bowker, 1967.

"Contemporary Classics for Young Adults." Chicago: ALA, 1985 (reprinted from July, 1985 *Booklist*).

"Contemporary Non-Fiction for Young Adults." *Booklist* (January 1, 1986)

Edwards, Margaret A. *The Fair Garden and the Swarm of Beasts: The Library and the Young Adult*. New York: Hawthorn, 1969.

Epstein, Connie C. "The Well-Read College-Bound Student." *School Library Journal* 30:32–35 (February 1984).

Gallo, Donald R., ed. *Books for You: A Booklist for Senior High School Students*. Rev. ed. Urbana, Ill.: National Council of Teachers of English, 1985.

Grosshans, Merilyn. "Booktalks as Bookbait." *School Library Media Quarterly* 11:127–33 (Winter 1983).

"Junior High Contemporary Classics." *Booklist* (December 15, 1984)

Moskowitz, Faye. "Why I Read to My Class." *New York Times: Education Life* (August 3, 1986), p. 62.

Moss, Elaine. "Reading and Writing: The Arithmetic." *Signal* 46: 22–26 (January 1985).

Nilsen, Alleen Pace, and Kenneth L. Donelson. *Literature for Today's Young Adults*. 2nd ed. Glenview, Ill.: Scott, Foresman, 1985.

Paulin, Mary Ann, and Susan Berlin, comps. *Outstanding Books for the College Bound*. Chicago: ALA, 1984.

Richler, Mordecai. "1944: The Year I Learned to Love a German." *New York Times Book Review* (February 2, 1986), p. 1.

Shapiro, Lillian L., ed. *Fiction for Youth: A Guide to Recommended Books*. 2nd ed. New York: Neal-Schuman, 1986.

Small, Robert C., Jr. "Some of My Favorite Books Are by Young Adult Authors and Some Are by Jane Austen." *English Journal* 75:81–84 (April 1986).

Stanek, Lou Willett. "Stunting Readers' Growth." *School Library Journal* 33:46–47 (November 1986).

Sutherland, Zena. *The Best in Children's Books: The University of Chicago Guide to Children's Literature, 1979–1984*. Chicago: Univ. of Chicago Pr., 1986.

"Young Adult Editors' Choice." *Booklist* (January 15). Annual.

Appendix:
Themes and Genres

Good books are not about one subject. Following are suggested categories, tentative and incomplete, that may help you in thinking about various themes and links for combining the titles in this book as well as those from your own wide reading.

Adventure (*see also* Science Fiction; Survival; War and peace)
Alive
Dove
Fantastic Voyage
The Guns of Navarone
Incident at Hawk's Hill
The Incredible Journey
The Island on Bird Street
The Kestrel
Lord of the Flies
"Love of Life"
The Sign of the Beaver
Slake's Limbo
"A Song in the Front Yard"
Survive the Savage Sea
Tracks
White Fang
Wolf of Shadows

Aging; intergenerational stories
Badger on the Barge, and Other Stories
Ceremony of Innocence
Doc

Gentlehands
Good Night, Mr. Tom
Homecoming
Howl's Moving Castle
I Know Why the Caged Bird Sings
The Nature of the Beast
One-Eyed Cat

Animals (*see also* chapter 5)
A Day No Pigs Would Die
"The Gift"
Island on Bird Street
"Love of Life"
Tex

The Arts
Annie on My Mind
Black Boy
The Course of True Love Never Did Run Smooth
Dragonsong
I Know Why the Caged Bird Sings
I Will Call It Georgie's Blues
In Summer Light
Midnight Hour Encores

Poetspeak
Prairie Songs
Remembering the Good Times
"Who Am I This Time?"

Biography
All Creatures Great and Small
(Herriot)
The Big Sea (Hughes)
Black Boy (Wright)
Boy (Dahl)
Diary of a Young Girl (Frank)
Dove (Graham)
Hunger of Memory (Rodriguez)
I Know Why the Caged Bird Sings
(Angelou)
Night (Wiesel)
Part of My Soul Went with Him
(Mandela)
Rain or Shine (McFadden)
"Ruth's Song (Because She Could
Not Sing It)" (Steinem)
The Woman Warrior (Kingston)
Zoo Vet (Taylor)

Cities
The Alfred Summer
Annie on My Mind
The Contender
The Keeper
"London"
Slake's Limbo
Underground

Country; small towns
All Creatures Great and Small
Ballad of the Sad Café
A Day No Pigs Would Die
A Fine White Dust
Half Nelson, Full Nelson
I Will Call It Georgie's Blues
In Country
A Place to Come Back To
A Summer to Die
Tex

Death and dying (*see also* Aging;
The Holocaust; War and peace)
A Day No Pigs Would Die
Doc
Father Figure
In Country
"Love of Life"
Ordinary People
Prairie Songs
Remembering the Good Times
"Song" ("When I Am Dead,
My Dearest")
A Summer to Die
Sweet Whispers, Brother Rush
We Have Always Lived in the Castle

Desolate setting
Ballad of the Sad Café
The Hound of the Baskervilles
The Incredible Journey
"Love of Life"
On the Edge
Prairie Songs
The Nature of the Beast
"Western Wind, When Wilt Thou
Blow?"
White Fang
Wuthering Heights

Disabled
Alan and Naomi
The Alfred Summer
The Ballad of the Sad Café
Flowers for Algernon
I Never Promised You a Rose
Garden
I Will Call It Georgie's Blues
In Country
Just One Friend
The Keeper
The Man without a Face
One Flew over the Cuckoo's Nest
Ordinary People
Prairie Songs
"Ruth's Song"
Sweet Whispers, Brother Rush

Tell Me That You Love Me,
  Junie Moon
Things Invisible to See

Family (*see also* Aging; Fathers;
  Mothers; Sisters and brothers)
Anastasia on Her Own
Boy
Early Sorrow
Family Resemblances
Famous All over Town
"The Gift"
Half Nelson, Full Nelson
I Will Call It Georgie's Blues
Love Lines
On the Edge
One-Eyed Cat
Ordinary People
Prairie Songs
Roll of Thunder, Hear My Cry
The Scarecrows
Wuthering Heights

Fantasy; horror
Beauty
The Changeover
A Christmas Carol
The Dark Is Rising
The Darkangel
Dragonsong
The Hero and the Crown
Howl's Moving Castle
"Nerves"
The Owl Service
The People Could Fly
Ratha's Creature
The Satanic Mill
The Scarecrows
Some Things Strange and Sinister
Sweet Whispers, Brother Rush
Things Invisible to See
"Thus I Refute Beelzy"
The Weirdstone of Brisingamen
Why Am I Grown So Cold?

Fathers
The Big Sea
The Catalogue of the Universe
The Chosen
A Day No Pigs Would Die
Famous All Over Town
Father Figure
Go Tell It on the Mountain
In Country
In Summer Light
The Keeper
Midnight Hour Encores
The Moonlight Man
One Fat Summer
Rain or Shine
The Runner
Summer of My German Soldier
"Those Winter Sundays"
"Thus I Refute Beelzy"
When I Whistle
Words by Heart

Friendship
Alan and Naomi
The Alfred Summer
Annie on My Mind
Bless the Beasts and Children
The Chosen
The Cruel Sea
Family Resemblances
Fast Sam, Cool Clyde, and Stuff
Finding David Dolores
I Love You, Stupid!
The Incredible Journey
Just One Friend
The Keeper
The Man without a Face
The Moves Make the Man
A Place to Come Back To
Remembering the Good Times
The Runner
The Sign of the Beaver
Summer of My German Soldier
Tell Me That You Love Me,
  Junie Moon

Gangs
The Chocolate War
The Contender
Famous All over Town
Fast Sam, Cool Clyde, and Stuff
Oliver Twist
Slake's Limbo

Historical fiction (*see also* The
   Holocaust; World War I; World
   War II)
Ask Me No Questions
Ceremony of Innocence
A Day No Pigs Would Die
The Fighting Ground
Flambards
Prairie Songs
Roll of Thunder, Hear My Cry
Sign of the Beaver
Tracks
Words by Heart

Holidays
A Christmas Carol
The Dark Is Rising
The Satanic Mill

The Holocaust
Alan and Naomi
Auschwitz
The Diary of a Young Girl
Gentlehands
The House on Prague Street
Island on Bird Street
Night

Humor
All Creatures Great and Small
Anastasia on Her Own
Animal Farm
"An Answer to the Parson"
Boy
Catch-22
A Christmas Carol
Famous All over Town
Fast Sam, Cool Clyde, and Stuff
The Flight of the Cassowary

Goodbye, Columbus
The Great Gilly Hopkins
Half Nelson, Full Nelson
The Hitchhiker's Guide to the
   Galaxy
Howl's Moving Castle
I Love You, Stupid!
The Norton Book of Light Verse
One Fat Summer
The Secret House
Slaughterhouse Five
"Song against Broccoli"
"Thus I Refute Beelzy"
Welcome to the Monkey-House
Zoo Vet

Journeys
About Time
American Classic
The Changeover
"The Doctor"
Dove
Dragonsong
Fantastic Voyage
The Fighting Ground
Freedom Rising
The Hitchhiker's Guide to the
   Galaxy
Homecoming
Immigrant Kids
The Incredible Journey
In Country
"Love of Life"
Midnight Hour Encores
The Moonlight Man
Oliver Twist
A Place to Come Back To
Pocket Poems
The Satanic Mill
Tracks
"The Ugly Little Boy"
Wolf of Shadows

Love (*see also* chapter 7)
Annie John
Boy

The Changeover
A Farewell to Arms
Finding David Dolores
"Frankie and Johnny"
I Know Why the Caged Bird Sings
I Will Call It Georgie's Blues
Love Is like the Lion's Tooth
The Moonlight Man
Rebecca
A Summer to Die
Tex

Men; cultural roles
Doc
Father Figure
Half Nelson, Full Nelson
I Love You, Stupid!
The Keeper
The Man without a Face
The Moves Make the Man
One Fat Summer
Remembering the Good Times
Running Loose
Tex

Minorities (*see also* The Holocaust;
World cultures)
Alan and Naomi (Jews)
The Big Sea (blacks)
Black Boy (blacks)
Ceremony of Innocence (Native
Americans)
The Chosen (Jews)
The Contender (blacks)
The Disappearance (blacks)
Famous All over Town (Hispanics)
Fast Sam, Cool Clyde, and Stuff
(blacks)
Go Tell It on the Mountain (blacks)
Goodbye, Columbus (Jews)
The House of Dies Drear (blacks)
Hunger of Memory (Hispanics)
I Am the Darker Brother (blacks)
I Know Why the Caged Bird Sings
(blacks)
I Love You, Stupid! (Jews)

The Moves Make the Man (blacks)
The People Could Fly (blacks)
Roll of Thunder, Hear My Cry
(blacks)
Sign of the Beaver (Native
Americans)
Summer of My German Soldier
(Jews)
Sweet Whispers, Brother Rush
(blacks)
The Woman Warrior (Asians)
Words by Heart (blacks)

Mothers
Annie John
Boy
The Catalogue of the Universe
Ceremony of Innocence
Finding David Dolores
The Great Gilly Hopkins
"Ruth's Song"
Sweet Whispers, Brother Rush

Mysteries; thrillers
Are You in the House Alone?
Be Buried in the Rain
The Disappearance
The Hound of the Baskervilles
The House of Dies Drear
The Machine Gunners
1984
On the Edge
Rebecca
The Scarecrows
Tracks
We Have Always Lived in the Castle
When No One Was Looking

Nonfiction (*see also* Biography;
Photographs and illustrations)
Ain't Gonna Study War No More
Alive
The Amateurs
Auschwitz
Creations
Crossing the Line

Day One
Dove
Freedom Rising
Gorillas in the Mist
Hiroshima
In the Shadow of Man
Outrageous Acts and Everyday
    Rebellions
The Secret House
Survive the Savage Sea

Nuclear War
Day One
Hiroshima
Wolf of Shadows

Orphans; foster children
Ask Me No Questions
Great Expectations
The Great Gilly Hopkins
Jane Eyre
Oliver Twist
The Queen's Gambit
Slake's Limbo

Outsiders (*see also* Minorities;
    Disabled)
Annie on My Mind
Beauty
Bless the Beasts and Children
The Chocolate War
"The Doctor"
Dragonsong
Frankenstein
Great Expectations
The Great Gilly Hopkins
Jane Eyre
The Loneliness of the Long-Distance
    Runner
1984
"No Man Is an Island"
Oliver Twist
One Fat Summer
The Queen's Gambit
Slake's Limbo
"The Ugly Little Boy"

Words by Heart
Wuthering Heights

Photographs and illustrations
Black Child
Castle
Children of the Wild West
Frankenstein
Immigrant Kids
Spaceshots
Underground

Poetry (*see also* chapter 2)
"An Answer to the Parson"
"Dulce et Decorum Est"
"The Gift"
Love Is like the Lion's Tooth
Love Lines
Norton Anthology of Light Verse
Poetspeak
"Snake"
"Western Wind, When Wilt Thou
    Blow?"

Quick talks
Are You in the House Alone?
The Changeover
The Dark Is Rising
Fantastic Voyage
Finding David Dolores
The Hitchhiker's Guide to the
    Galaxy
Just One Friend
The Machine Gunners
The Sign of the Beaver
Slake's Limbo
Sweet Whispers, Brother Rush
"The Ugly Little Boy"
We Have Always Lived in the Castle

Religion and philosophy
Alan and Naomi
The Catalogue of the Universe
Ceremony of Innocence
The Chosen
A Christmas Carol

Creations
A Day No Pigs Would Die
A Fine White Dust
Ge Tell It on the Mountain
I Will Call It Georgie's Blues
Lord of the Flies
"No Man Is an Island"
Story for a Black Night
Words by Heart

Runaways
A Fine White Dust
Half Nelson, Full Nelson
Homecoming
Oliver Twist
Slake's Limbo
Tracks

School
Boy
The Chocolate War
Crossing the Line
Just One Friend
Remembering the Good Times
A Separate Peace

Science fiction
About Time
"Caught in the Organ Draft"
Creations
"The Doctor"
Ender's Game
Fantastic Voyage
Flowers for Algernon
Frankenstein
The Hitchhiker's Guide to the
   Galaxy
1984
Slaughterhouse Five
"The Sound Machine"
"The Ugly Little Boy"
Welcome to the Monkey-House
"The Winner"
Wolf of Shadows

Secret houses
Ballad of the Sad Café
Be Buried in the Rain
A Fine White Dust
Great Expectations
The Hound of the Baskervilles
The House of Dies Drear
I Will Call It Georgie's Blues
Jane Eyre
On the Edge
One-Eyed Cat
Rebecca
The Secret House
Sirens and Spies
Wuthering Heights

Short stories
About Time
Badger on the Barge, and other
   Stories
Caught in the Organ Draft
"The Doctor"
Early Sorrow
The Loneliness of the Long-Distance
   Runner
"Long Walk to Forever"
"Love of Life"
"Nerves"
"The Sound Machine"
"Thus I Refute Beelzy"
"The Ugly Little Boy"
"Who Am I This Time?"
"The Winner"

Sisters and brothers
The Changeover
Don't Blame the Music
Father Figure
Homecoming
I Know Why the Caged Bird Sings
I Will Call It Georgie's Blues
Jacob Have I Loved
The Man without a Face
A Summer to Die
Sweet Whispers, Brother Rush
Tex

Sports
The Amateurs
The Chosen
The Contender
Half Nelson, Full Nelson
The Loneliness of the Long-Distance
 Runner
The Moves Make the Man
Running Loose
Things Invisible to See
When No One Was Looking

Substance abuse
The Contender
The Moonlight Man
The Queen's Gambit

Survival (*see also* chapter 6;
 The Holocaust, War and peace)
Black Boy
The Chocolate War
Escape from Warsaw
Fantastic Voyage
Homecoming
Slake's Limbo
Tracks
White Fang
Wolf of Shadows
The Woman Warrior

Terror (*see also* chapters 2 and 8)
Boy
The Darkangel
Frankenstein
The Hound of the Baskervilles
Oliver Twist
We Have Always Lived in the Castle
Why Am I Grown So Cold?

War and peace (*see also* chapter 4)
Black Boy
The Kestrel
Lord of the Flies
One-Eyed Cat
White Fang

Women; cultural roles
Annie on My Mind
Beauty
The Bride Price
Ceremony of Innocence
The Darkangel
Dragonsong
Family Resemblances
Finding David Dolores
The Hero and the Crown
I Know Why the Caged Bird Sings
In Country
The Moonlight Man
Outrageous Acts and Everyday
 Rebellions
Part of My Soul Went with Him
Prairie Songs
The Queen's Gambit
Ratha's Creature
Sirens and Spies
The Woman Warrior

World cultures (*see also* The
 Holocaust; World War I; World
 War II)
Annie John (Caribbean)
Black Child (South Africa)
The Bride Price (Nigeria)
The Catalogue of the Universe
 (New Zealand)
The Changeover (New Zealand)
Crossing the Line (South Africa)
Freedom Rising (South Africa)
From the Country of Eight Islands
 (Japan)
"Nerves" (France)
Love Is like the Lion's Tooth
 (world)
Part of My Soul Went with Him
 (South Africa)
Poems of Black Africa
The Satanic Mill (Germany)
A Simple Lust (South Africa)
Story for a Black Night (Liberia)
When I Whistle (Japan)

Why Am I Grown So Cold? (world)
The Yellow Canary Whose Eye Is So
  Black (Latin America)
Zero Makes Me Hungry (world)

World War I
Ain't Gonna Study War No More
All Quiet on the Western Front
"Dulce et Decorum Est"
A Farewell to Arms
Flambards
No Hero for the Kaiser

World War II (*see also* The
  Holocaust; Nuclear war; War and
  peace)
Alan and Naomi
Catch-22
The Cruel Sea
Escape from Warsaw
Fireweed
Good Night, Mr. Tom
The Guns of Navarone
The Machine Gunners
Sirens and Spies
Slaughterhouse Five

Index

Prepared by Gene Heller